D0688268

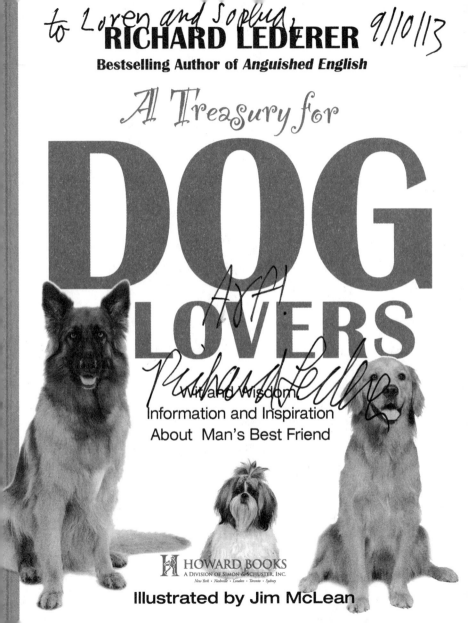

to Loren and Sophia,
RICHARD LEDERER 9/10/13

Bestselling Author of *Anguished English*

A Treasury for

DOG

LOVERS

Wit and Wisdom,
Information and Inspiration
About Man's Best Friend

H **HOWARD BOOKS**
A DIVISION OF SIMON & SCHUSTER, INC.
New York • Nashville • London • Toronto • Sydney

Illustrated by Jim McLean

Our purpose at Howard Books is to:
Increase faith in the hearts of growing Christians
Inspire holiness in the lives of believers
Instill hope in the hearts of struggling people everywhere
Because He's coming again!

Published by Howard Books, a division of Simon & Schuster, Inc.
1230 Avenue of the Americas, New York, NY 10020
www.howardpublishing.com

A Treasury for Dog Lovers © 2009 by Richard Lederer

All rights reserved, including the right to reproduce this book or portions thereof in any form whatsoever. For information, address Howard Subsidiary Rights Department, 1230 Avenue of the Americas, New York, NY 10020.

Library of Congress Cataloging-in-Publication Data is available.

ISBN 978-1-4391-0315-9

10 9 8 7 6 5 4 3

HOWARD and colophon are registered trademarks of Simon & Schuster, Inc.

Manufactured in the United States of America

For information regarding special discounts for bulk purchases, please contact: Simon & Schuster Special Sales at 1-866-506-1949 or business@simonandschuster.com.

The Simon & Schuster Speakers Bureau can bring authors to your live event. For more information or to book an event contact the Simon & Schuster Speakers Bureau at 1-866-248-3049 or visit our website at www.simonspeakers.com.

Edited by Chrys Howard
Cover and interior design by Stephanie D. Walker
Illustrations by James McLean

To our dear friends, Bart and Mike—
beauty without vanity,
strength without insolence,
courage without ferocity

Acknowledgments

The verb *to vet* means "to examine credentials, manuscripts, or other documents as a veterinarian examines an animal, hoping to give it a clean bill of health." I thank the staff of the San Diego Humane Society for vetting the text of this treasury to ensure that the facts are accurate and the tone sensitive.

I also thank Bob Vetere of the American Pet Products Association for vetting the data in the Introduction.

I have striven mightily to track down the source of every item in this book that isn't of my own making. To those creators whom I have not been able to identify, I hope you are pleased that your luminous contributions gleam, albeit anonymously, from these pages.

Contents

Contents

Introduction

**Dogs are not our whole life,
but they make our lives whole.**
—Roger Caras

The United States is a nation of dog lovers. About 77 million dogs live here, and more than 6 million Canine Americans are born here each year. More than one in three American families (39 percent) own a dog, the highest dog population in the world.

Our mass caninophilia (love of dogs) speaks volumes about America. "The greatness of a nation and its moral progress," said Mahatma Gandhi, "can be measured by the way in which its animals are treated." Six out of every ten American households are graced by pets, whereas only three of every ten have children. Each year we spend more than $43 billion on our pets, including $8 billion on dog food and $4 billion on cat food, more than we spend on baby food. Based on a dog's average life span of eleven years, the cost of owning a dog is $13,350.

In our nation, 91 percent of dog owners speak baby talk to their dogs and buy them gifts. According to other surveys, 70 percent of people sign their pet's name on greeting and holiday cards, and 58 percent include pets in family and holiday portraits. An American Animal Hospital Association poll found that 33 percent of dog owners admit to talking to their dogs on the phone and leaving answering machine messages for them while away.

An estimated one million dogs in America have been named as primary beneficiaries in their owners' wills. In 2007, hotel heiress Leona Helmsley left $12 million to her dog, a white Maltese named Trouble.

Why do we love thee, doggies? Let us count the ways. Dogs are highly companionable, obedient, and playful animals. No other creature on earth shares our homes and our lives the way dogs do. The partnership is unique in interspecies relationships. The loyalty and devotion that dogs demonstrate as part of their natural pack-animal instincts exemplifies the human idea of love and friendship. Dogs seem to view their humans as members of their pack, and the same goes for most dog owners. To us, dogs are adopted sons and daughters who are short, hairy, walk on all fours, and possess rudimentary speech.

Dogs show us our finest selves. The romantic poet Lord Byron wrote on the tomb of his Newfoundland: "Near this spot are deposited the remains of one who possessed beauty without vanity, strength without insolence, courage without ferocity, and all the virtues of man, without his vices. This praise, which would be unmeaning flattery if inscribed over human ashes, is but a just tribute to the memory of Boatswain, a dog."

Think about it. We give dogs what time we can spare, what space we can spare, what food we can spare, and what love we can spare. In return, dogs give us their all. It's the best deal we human beings have ever made. The least we lucky dog lovers can do is write a book in praise of our best friends. This is that book.

If you can be cheerful, ignoring aches and pains;

If you can resist complaining and boring people with your troubles;

If you can eat the same food every day and be grateful for it;

If you can understand when loved ones are too busy to give you any time;

If you can take criticism and blame without resentment;

If you can relax without liquor and sleep without the aid of drugs;

If you can face the world without lies and deceit;

If you can start the day without caffeine or pep pills;

If you can find great happiness in the simplest things in life;

If you can forgive any action in the blink of an eye;

If you can repel intruders without using lethal weapons;

If you have no bias against creed, color, religion, politics, or gender;

If you offer unconditional love as naturally as you breathe;

... then you are almost as good as your dog.

Richard Lederer
San Diego, California
richard.lederer@pobox.com

1 Are You a Dog Lover?

Properly trained, a man can be a dog's best friend.
—*Corey Ford*

It's sad how dogs, those most loyal and companionable of creatures, are treated so shabbily in our English language. It's easy to think of common words and expressions that are negative about dogs—*hangdog, underdog, dog tired, a dog's life, you dirty dog, sick as a dog, in the doghouse, you're dogging it, going to the dogs, you're dogmeat*—on and on it goes. But why don't we say *cute as a dog, amiable as a dog, loyal as a dog, loving as a dog*? How many positive canine words and phrases leap to mind? Not many.

Nonetheless, there are numerous men and women perambulating the earth—in appearance much like ordinary, respectable citizens—who have warm, passionate feelings about dogs. These are dog people, and they are a special breed not recognized by the American Kennel Club.

You know you're a dog lover if . . .

- You can't go more than a half hour without the urge to pat a furry head.

- You feel strangely powerful knowing that even your smallest smile can set your pet's tail thumping.

- You can't wait to arrive home so you will be greeted by shining, liquid eyes and a tap-dancing frenzy of fur.

- There is no sweeter sound to your ears than a doggie pleasure grunt.

- All of your clothes have dog hair on them, even when they come back from the Laundromat or dry cleaner's. Dog hair is everywhere— on your rug, your bedspread, your packing tape, and in your sinks. Even when you find a dog hair in your food, you remove it and blithely go on eating.

- Lintrollers are on your shopping list every week.

- When you are cold, you put a sweater on your dog.

- Your floors are littered with rawhide bones and dog toys. You have five squeaky hedgehogs, but only one with a squeaky that actually works.

- You have no small children at home, but you have permanent baby gates installed in strategic doorways and a kiddy wading pool in the yard.

- You refer to yourself as "Mommy" or "Daddy."

- You often talk in a goofy high voice.

- Your vet's receptionist recognizes your voice. That's because when you and your dog get sick, you take the dog to the vet's but settle for an over-the-counter remedy for yourself.

- The instructions to the dog kennel are longer than the instructions to the house sitter.

- When you send friends and families cards, you sign for your dog. On your Christmas cards appears a photograph of your dog wearing fake reindeer antlers.

- You keep a mental list of people you would like to spay or neuter. You like people who like your dog and despise people who don't.

- You absentmindedly pat people on the head or scratch them behind their ears.
- You tell your children to "Heel!" in a grocery store.
- You know the names of all the dogs who regularly play in the dog park, but you don't know the names of most of their owners.
- City officials come to your home and say, "Your dogs are barking"—and you can't figure out what the problem is.
- It's easier to get a hairdresser's appointment for yourself than it is to get one for your dog.
- You go to the pet supply store every Saturday because it's one of the very few places that lets you bring your dog inside, and your dog loves to go with you.
- You carry dog treats in your pocket or purse at all times.
- You cringe at the rising price of food in the grocery store but think nothing of the cost of dog food or treats.
- You think nothing of spending $500 on gas, $200 on a motel room, and $150 for meals to bring home a 35¢ prize ribbon.
- In your photo album there is scarcely a picture of anybody with two legs.
- Your dog is the star of your Web site.
- Your front passenger-side windshield and side-view mirror are festooned with doggie noseprints.

- Your dog's name is featured on your license plate or license-plate holder.

- You love bringing home doggie bags. You never completely finish a piece of steak or chicken or fish so your dog gets a taste, too.

- Nobody's feet are allowed on the furniture, but your dogs are welcome to sleep on any piece they so choose.

- You not only allow dogs on the couch; guests have to sit on the floor because the dog has "territorial issues."

- You always carry a plastic bag—just in case.

- Your parents refer to your pet as their granddog.

- The first question you ask when on a date is: "So, do you like dogs?"

- Every chance you get, you lecture people on responsible dog ownership.

- When you leave home, you pat your spouse on the head and kiss your dog goodbye.

- If you're an author, you dedicate your books to your dogs. I dedicate this book to Bart and Mike, the sprightly and companionable black Lab mixes with whom my wife Simone and I have the honor of sharing our lives.

2 Fascinating Facts About Dogs

GULLIVER ?

All knowledge,
the totality of all questions
and answers,
is contained in the dog.

—*Franz Kafka*

Dogs, wolves, and foxes are descended from a small, weasel-like mammal called *Miacis*, a tree-dwelling creature that existed about forty million years ago. Scientists have discovered 400,000-year-old wolf bones mingled with human bones. Dogs were first domesticated from wolves and bred at least seventeen thousand years ago, perhaps even 150,000 years ago, based upon recent genetic fossil and DNA evidence.

Written records more than four thousand years old from China show that dog trainers were held in high esteem and that kennel masters raised and looked after large numbers of dogs. Being mummified was an honor in ancient Egypt. Archeologists have discovered hundreds of dog mummies buried in many cemeteries from Abydos to Saqqâra.

Over time, the dog has developed into more than four hundred breeds, characterized by an almost infinite variety. The Saint Bernard is the heaviest, tipping the scale up to two hundred pounds. The weightiest—and longest—dog ever recorded was an Old English Mastiff named Zorba, who weighed in at 343 pounds and measured eight feet three inches from nose to tail.

The tallest dogs are the Great Dane and the Irish wolfhound (thirty-nine inches at the shoulder). Gibson, a mammoth Great Dane from

California, stood more than three and a half feet tall at the shoulder.

The world's smallest dog breeds are the Chihuahua (shortest in length) and the Yorkshire terrier (shortest in height). The teeniest dog on record was a Yorkshire terrier owned by Arthur Maples of Blackburn, England. This particular dog was two and a half inches high at the shoulder, three and three quarters inches long from the tip of its nose to the root of its tail, and weighed four ounces. It died in 1945.

Colors range from white to black, with reds, grays, and browns occurring in a tremendous variation of patterns. The Yorkshire terrier has hair that can be two feet long, while other breeds may have no hair at all, such as the Mexican Hairless. Dogs are the most diverse mammal on earth. No other creature comes with even a quarter of the variety of sizes, shapes, and features:

> Some dogs are tall. Some dogs are small.
> Some skinny, some beefy, some burly.
> Some dogs are petite, and some are fleet.
> Some hairless, some fluffy, some curly.
>
> Some dogs are long. Some dogs are strong.
> Some flat-faced, some wrinkly, some jowly.
> Some have a snout that sticks way out,
> Some yippy, some arfy, some howly.
>
> By dappled and brindled our hearts are enkindled,
> By gray and by brown and by white.
> By spots and by splatters and infinite patterns,
> By dogs as black as night.

Such a kaleidoscope of canine bodies occurs because dogs possess "elastic genes" that have come into play as we have bred them for so many different tasks. Dogs were originally domesticated for their usefulness in hunting, herding, hauling, pest control, and keeping watch.

It may be difficult to "teach an old dog new tricks," but dogs have in fact been trained to perform highly skilled tasks, such as turning a spit holding meat over an open fire; guiding the blind; serving as companions for the disabled; sniffing out illegal drugs, bombs, counterfeit money, cancer, or cadavers; collecting birds' eggs in their mouths without breaking the shells; locating truffles; running races; acting in movies, plays, and TV shows; traveling in space; and competing to be Best in Show.

In many countries, the most common and perhaps most important role of dogs is as companion. Dogs have lived with and worked with humans in so many roles that their loyalty has earned them the unique sobriquet "man's best friend." In fact, studies show that owning a dog alleviates loneliness, anxiety, and depression; reduces stress, high blood pressure, and heart disease; and adds six months to the average person's life.

Here are more fascinating facts about our best friends:

- There is only a 0.2 percent difference between the mitochondrial DNA of a dog and the mitochondrial DNA of a gray wolf.

- The average life span for mixed-breed and midsize dogs is thirteen to fourteen years. In general, larger breeds have shorter life spans. Many giant dog breeds average eight to ten years, while some small terrier breeds might live as long as twenty years. The average city dog lives three years longer than a country dog. The oldest reliable age recorded for a dog is twenty-nine years, five months, for a Queensland "heeler" named Bluey, who died in 1939 in Victoria, Australia.

- A one-year-old dog is physically as mature as a fifteen-year-old human. Smaller breeds of dogs mature faster than larger breeds.

- The domestic dog is very similar to the wild dog in practically everything, except for barking. Domestic dogs and wild dogs can all breed with one another and produce healthy young puppies. Their bodies are quite similar, and they even have a similar vocal repertoire. They can whine, snarl, howl, or growl—and they can also bark. Both wild and domestic dog puppies and wolves will vocalize, but only the domestic dog will bark in machine-gun bursts—*rau-rau-rau-rau, rau-rau-rau, rau-rau-rau-rau-rau*. Wolves and wild dogs do not eject that powerful stream of staccato decibels. One cocker spaniel was clocked at 907 barks in just ten minutes.

- The average litter size is five puppies. In rare cases, litters of more than twenty have been recorded. A female dog carries her young about sixty days before the puppies are born. If never spayed or neutered, a female dog, her mate, and their puppies could, in theory, produce more than 66,000 dogs in six years.

- Puppies do not begin wagging their tails until they are about a month old.

- Dogs are omnivorous. They need more than just meat to flourish.

- Mixed-breed dogs usually have behavioral traits similar to the breed they most resemble in appearance. But the physical characteristics of a mixed-breed dog can come as a complete surprise.

- Many experts confirm what most dog owners believe—that dogs actually smile. Perhaps they have learned to curl their black doggie lips into a grin in order to mimic the human smile as an expression of joy.

- When a dog bays at the moon or at a passing siren, it is following a basic urge to call the pack together.

- The burying of bones is part of a dog's instinctive feeding ritual. Shaking things viciously is part of the hunting ritual.

- Dogs and cats turn in circles before lying down because in the wild this instinctive action turns long grass into a bed.

- Chocolate contains a substance known as theobromine (similar to caffeine) that stimulates the central nervous system and the heart. Ingested in large quantities, chocolate can sicken or kill dogs. And please be aware that a single Tylenol can kill a dog.

- The Girl Scouts and the Boy Scouts both offer merit badges in dog care.

- The Bible mentions dogs fourteen times, the domestic cat not once.

- Three dogs survived the sinking of the Titanic—a Newfoundland, a Pomeranian, and a Pekingese. They escaped on early lifeboats carrying so few people that no one objected.

- At the end of World War I, the German government trained the first guide dogs to assist blind war veterans. The first seeing-eye dog in the United States was presented to a blind person on April 25, 1938.

- U.S. drug-sniffing customs dogs, Rocky and Barco, were so good at patrolling the border that Mexican drug lords put a $30,000 bounty on their heads.

All I Need to Know 3
I Learned from My Dog

> For a dog, every morning is
> Christmas morning.
> Every walk is the best walk,
> every meal is the best meal,
> every game is the best game.
> —*Cesar Millan*

> A dog teaches a boy fidelity, perseverance,
> and to turn around three times before lying down.
> —*Robert Benchley*

- Live for the moment. Enjoy the simple things in life, like taking a long walk or riding in a car and feeling the wind blowing on your face.
- Take time to stop and eat the roses.
- Trust your instincts.
- If you stare at someone long enough, eventually you'll get what you want.
- Don't go out without ID.
- When loved ones come home, always run to greet them.
- Be direct with people; let them know exactly how you feel by piddling on their shoes.
- When it's in your best interest, practice obedience.
- Listen respectfully to what others have to say.
- Be aware of when to hold your tongue and when to use it.

- Master the art of stretching.
- Run barefoot, romp, and play daily. Leave yourself breathless at least once a day.
- On hot days, drink lots of water and lie under a shady tree.
- Eat with gusto and enthusiasm.
- Be loyal.
- Never pretend to be something you're not.
- Know all the sunny places.
- Life is hard, and then you nap.
- Sneeze unabashedly.
- Flaunt your hair loss.
- Let others know when they've invaded your territory.
- Make your mark on the world as much as you can.
- When you do something wrong, always take responsibility (as soon as you're dragged out from under the bed).
- If it's not wet and sloppy, it's not a real kiss.
- When someone is having a bad day, be silent, sit close by, and nuzzle them gently.
- Thrive on attention and let people touch you.
- Avoid biting when a simple growl will do.
- When you're happy, dance around and wag your entire body.
- To err is human; to forgive canine.
- No matter how often you're scolded, don't buy into the guilt thing and pout. Run right back and make friends.

The Dog's Got Our Tongue 4

In order to really enjoy a dog,
one doesn't merely try to train him
to be semi-human.
The point of it is to open oneself
to the possibility
of becoming partly a dog.
—*Edward Hoagland*

The word *dog* trots, prances, scampers, and barks through our marvelous English language. We call a tenacious person a bulldog, a showoff a hot dog, a fortunate person a lucky dog, a man with an active social life a gay dog who puts on the dog ("makes a flashy display"), and a rapscallion a cur or dirty dog. A dominant person is a top dog who can run with the big dogs, while his counterpart is an underdog. Some of us lead a dog's life going to the dogs in the doghouse. Others are young pups in puppy love.

One of the most endearing characteristics of dogs is fidelity to their owners, which has made dogs valued companions. As long ago as 1150, the learned St. Bernard of Clairvaux said, "*Qui me amat, amat et canem meam.*" That translates to "Love me, love my dog"—an expression of unconditional affection that reposes in many languages. That's a *dog-eared* phrase, so-called because a page in a well-worn book can get folded over like the ear of a dog.

Other canine proverbs yip and bark across centuries. In Geoffrey Chaucer's fourteenth-century tale of *Troilus and Creseyde,* the poet writes, "It is nought good a sleping hound to wake," which comes down to us as "Let sleeping dogs lie."

15

Another expression derived from literature is, believe it or not, "in the doghouse," which means out of favor with the powers that be. The first appearance of this phrase occurs in James Barrie's play *Peter Pan* (1904). Mr. Darling, the father of the three children, is punished for his shabby treatment of Nana, the Newfoundland dog, who is also the children's nurse. And where does he spend his exile? In Nana's doghouse, of course.

There abound a number of explanations for *it's raining cats and dogs*, including the fact that felines and canines were closely associated with the rain and wind in northern mythology. In Odin days, dogs were often pictured as the attendants of Odin, the storm god, and cats were believed to cause storms. Another theory posits that during heavy rains in seventeenth-century England, some city streets became raging rivers of filth carrying many drowned cats and dogs. But the truth appears to be more mundane. Cats and dogs make a lot of noise when they fight (hence, "fighting like cats and dogs"), so they have become a metaphor for a noisy rain or thunderstorm.

Sometimes dogs fight with other dogs over a single bone, a scene that gives us the phrase *bone of contention*. This transfer of a canine quarrel to a human quarrel began as a *bone of dissension:* "This became a bone of dissension between these deere friends," William Lambarde, 1576.

A *three-dog night* is not only a popular music group of the 1970s, but a night so cold that one must sleep with three dogs in order to generate enough body heat to be comfortable.

Dog eat dog dates from the sixteenth century, even though Marcus Teretius Varro reminded us in 43 B.C. that "*Canis caninam non est*"—"Dogs are not cannibals." Even older is the proverbial "dog in a manger," from an Aesop's fable written around 570 B.C. about a snarling dog who prevents oxen from eating their corn, even though the dog doesn't want it for himself.

In the days of the Romans, the six or eight hottest weeks of the summer were known colloquially as *caniculares dies,* or "days of the dog." The Romans believed that during the period roughly from July 3 to August 11, the dog star Sirius rose with and added its heat to the sun, making it the hottest time of year.

In the early nineteenth-century in American English, *barker* came to signify the person who stands outside a carnival or circus to shout (bark) out its attractions to passersby. From the same period in America arose the expression "to bark up the wrong tree," from hunting dogs that mistakenly crowd around the base of a tree thinking they have treed a raccoon that has actually taken a different route. The phrase is still used to mean wasting one's energy by pursuing the wrong path.

Another classic Americanism is *hot dog*. In the nineteenth-century United States, some folks suspected that sausages were made from dog meat, as evidenced by this popular ditty:

> Oh where, oh where has my little dog gone?
> Oh where, oh where can he be?
> Now sausage is good, baloney, of course.
> Oh where, oh where can he be?
> They make them of dog, they make them of horse.
> I think they made them of he.

When hot sausages in a bun became popular, it was but a short leap to the term *hot dog*. Cartoonist Tad Dorgan featured the hot dog in some of his sports cartoons, helping to popularize the new name. That the sausage looks a little like the body of a dachshund also helped the *hot dog* to cleave to the American palate.

From what creature did the Canary Islands derive their name? Dogs, of course. The Canary Islands were named after the large dogs *(canes grandes)* found there. The familiar yellow songbirds, also native creatures thereabouts, were named after the islands, rather than the other way around.

We could talk about dogs in our language until the last dog is hung. Here the reference is to the dirty dog of the human species who rustled your cattle, and the "hung" is to the vigilante lynchings known as "necktie parties" in the early West. Nowadays the expression most often points to the inevitable two or three people at every party who hang around everlastingly—until the last dog is hung and the host shows them to the door.

Find the Hidden Dogs 5

Watch out or my karma
will run over your dogma.
—*Author Unknown*

Here are some statements about canines hiding in our language. In some cases, the dog in a word or phrase barks clearly, as in *dog days*. In other cases, a word or phrase bears no relationship to the word *dog* beyond a mere coincidence of sound. But each word or word grouping in the game you are about to play does begin with the letters *d-o-g*, and these letters are pronounced exactly like the name of the animal.

Find the hidden dogs. Answers follow.

1. This dog is an established set of beliefs. _____

2. This dog is another word for "darn." _____

3. This dog is a stretch of land that bends. _____

4. This dog swims underwater. _____

5. This dog is an elementary form of swimming. _____

6. L'il Abner lived in this dog. _____

7. This dog writes clumsy verse. _____

8. This dog is shabby and worn. _____

9. This dog is exhausted. _____

10. This dog is a poisonous plant. _____

11. This dog is used for identification. _____

12. This dog is up a tree. _____

13. This dog is also up a tree. _____

14. This dog is a quick, easy gait. _____

15. This dog is a fiercely disputed contest. _____

Answers

1. dogma 2. doggone 3. dogleg 4. dogfish 5. dog paddle 6. Dogpatch
7. doggerel 8. dog-eared 9. dog tired 10. dogbane 11. dog tag 12. dogberry
13. dogwood 14. dogtrot 15. dogfight

The Body Canine 6

The eyes of a dog,
the expression of a dog,
the warmly wagging tail of a dog,
and the gloriously cold, damp nose
of a dog were, in my opinion,
all God-given for one purpose
only—to make complete fools
of us human beings.

—*Barbara Woodhouse*

They say animal behavior can warn you when an earthquake
is coming. Like the night before that last earthquake hit,
our family dog took the car keys and drove to Arizona.

—*Bob Hope*

- All dogs—from the gigantic to the miniature, from the most exquisitely pedigreed show animal to the humblest mixed breed mutt—are identical in anatomy, with 321 bones and forty-two permanent teeth. They can all breed together and produce fertile offspring. They are all of the same species.

- Dogs' eyes have large pupils and a wide field of vision, making them highly adept at following moving objects. Any ball-tossing, Frisbee-throwing owner will affirm that observation, as well as the fact that dogs also see well in low light.

- It is a myth that dogs are color-blind. They can actually see in color, just not as vividly as humans. It is akin to our vision at dusk. Dogs are able to see much better in dim light than humans are. This is due to the *tapetum lucidum*, a light-reflecting layer behind the retina. Because it functions like a mirror, it also accounts for the strange shine or glow in a dog's eyes at night.

- A dog's nose is kept moist by fluid from a gland inside the nose. This moisture helps him detect odors by capturing and dissolving molecules of scent, even scents up to two weeks old. Dogs have a formidable sense of smell, a thousand times more powerful than a human's. Dogs have many more olfactory cells than our 5,000,000. A dachshund has 125,000,000, a fox terrier 147,000,000, and an Alsatian (often used as a "sniffer" dog) 220,000,000. If you unfolded and laid out the delicate membranes from inside a dog's nose, the membranes would be larger than the dog itself.

- A dog's noseprints are as unique as a human's fingerprints and can be used to accurately identify each animal.

- Dogs have twice as many muscles for moving their ears as do people. Dogs' sense of hearing is more than ten times more acute than ours. Using their swiveling ears like radar dishes, dogs can hear sounds 250 yards away that most people cannot hear beyond twenty-five yards. The human ear can detect sound waves vibrating at frequencies up to twenty thousand times a second. But dogs can hear sound waves that vibrate at frequencies of more than thirty thousand times a second. A dog can distinguish the unique footfall of his master and the unique sound of the family car at considerable distances. These skills are the legacy of ancestral wolves, who could hear a howl from a distance of at least four miles.

- The mouth of the average dog exerts 150 to 200 pounds of pressure per square inch. Some dogs can apply up to 450 pounds.

- Ever notice that your dog prefers to "shake" with the same paw each time? According to tests made at the Institute for the Study of Animal Problems, in Washington, D.C., dogs and cats, like people, are either right-handed or left-handed. That is, they favor either their right or left paws.

- The higher the tail, the more confident the dog. A dominant dog will hold his tail straight up or just slightly curved over his back.

- Contrary to popular belief, dogs do not sweat by panting and salivating. The only sweat glands dogs possess are located between their paw pads. The only way they can discharge heat is by panting. While panting, a dog will moisten its ginormous tongue to increase evaporation.

- At birth, puppies are deaf, blind, and have almost no sense of smell. They stay near their mother and siblings because of the warmth. A puppy's eyes do not open until it is ten to fifteen days old. Its vision is usually not completely developed until it is about four weeks old.

- A dog's heart beats between seventy and 120 times a minute. A human heart beats seventy to eighty times a minute.

- The normal body temperature for a dog is 101.2 degrees Fahrenheit.

- Some dogs are so strong that they can pull loads of more than five thousand pounds.

- Parts of a dog's body have been identified with intriguing names:

    Brisket—The chest of the dog

    Carpals—The wrist, the bones of the lower legs

Dewclaw—The tiny, useless, fifth claw, located on the inner part of the leg above the other toes

Flews—The hanging part of the dog's upper lips

Hock—The bones that form the ankle/heel of the dog

Muzzle—The front parts of the jaws

Pastern—The part of the leg below the knee of the front leg or below the hock of the hind leg

Ruff—The long, thick hair that grows around the neck

Stifle—The knee, located on the hind leg above the ankle

Stop—The indented part of the skull between the eyes

Withers—The top of the shoulders, just behind the neck

Lucky Dogs 7

I think we are drawn
to dogs because they are
the uninhibited creatures
we might be if we weren't
certain we knew better.

—George Bird Evans

Here are two dozen reasons why it's great to be a dog:

1. Your friends never expect you to pay for lunch, dinner, or anything else for that matter.

2. When it's raining, you can lie around the house all day and never worry about being fired.

3. If it itches, you can reach it. And no matter where it itches, no one will be offended if you scratch it in public.

4. No one notices if you have hair growing in weird places as you get older.

5. Personal hygiene is a blast: No one expects you to take a bath every day, and you don't even have to comb your own hair.

6. You don't have to worry about table manners—and there's no such thing as bad food.

7. If you put on weight, it's somebody else's fault.

8. Having a wet nose is considered a sign of good health. Nobody asks you to wipe your wet nose.

9. No one thinks less of you for passing gas. Some people might actually think you're cute.

10. Who needs a big home entertainment system? A bone or an old shoe or a peanut butter jar can entertain you for hours.

11. You can spend hours just smelling stuff—and everything smells good.

12. If you're good at sniffing drugs, people value you even more.

13. It doesn't take much to make you happy. You're always excited to see the same old people. All they have to do is leave the room for five minutes and come back.

14. Every garbage can looks like a cold buffet or fast food stop to you.

15. It doesn't bother you if your favorite television show is a rerun.

16. You can wear fur and no one thinks you're insensitive.

17. April 15 means nothing to you.

18. You don't have to "amount to anything." All you have to do is be a dog.

19. The older you get, the more people respect you.

20. You can sleep late every day.

21. You never get in trouble for putting your head in a stranger's lap.

22. People think you're normal if you stick your head out the window to feel the wind in your hair.

23. Puppy love can last your whole life.

24. You have many friends because you wag your tail instead of your tongue.

A Doggie Dictionary 8

**Our perfect companions
never have fewer than four feet.**
—*Colette*

One could define the word *dog* as "a creature who wears his heart on his tail." Here's
a start on a dictionary to be read by dogs
themselves:

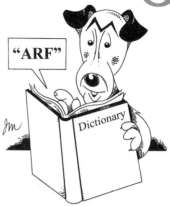

Ball. A spheroid that humans keep los-
ing and that you must always be sure
to track down and return to them.

Bath. A process by which the humans drench the floor, walls, and themselves. You can help by shaking vigorously and frequently.

Bicycle. A two-wheeled exercise machine, invented for dogs to control
body fat. To get maximum aerobic benefit, you must hide behind a
bush and dash out, bark loudly, and run alongside for a few yards;
the person then swerves and falls into the bushes, and you prance
away.

Bump. The best way to get your human's attention when they are drink-
ing a fresh cup of coffee or tea.

Cat Litter. A great place to go for a buffet dinner.

Children. Short humans of optimal petting height. Standing close to
one assures some great petting. When running, they are good to
chase. If they fall down, they are comfortable to sit on.

Deafness. A malady that affects dogs when their person wants them in and they want to stay out. Symptoms include staring blankly at the person, then running in the opposite direction, or lying down.

Dinner Table. That which you should sit under during mealtimes in order to catch falling scraps and hence doing your part to keep the home clean.

Dog Bed. Any soft, clean surface, such as the white bedspread in the guest room, the newly upholstered couch in the living room, or the dry-cleaning that was just picked up.

Dog Breath. That which makes a dog's bark worse than his bite.

Dogma. Canine mother.

Dogmatic. Runs on canine power.

Doorbell. A signal that dangerous people have come to your home. You must sound the alarm!

Drool. What you do when your humans have food and you don't. To drool properly, you must sit as close as you can, look sad, and let the drool fall to the floor, or better yet, on their laps.

Garbage Can. A container that your neighbors put out once a week to test your ingenuity. You must stand on your hind legs and try to push the lid off with your nose. If you do it right, you are rewarded with margarine wrappers to shred, beef bones to consume, moldy crusts of bread, and sometimes even an old sneaker.

Goose Bump. A maneuver to use as a last resort when the Regular Bump doesn't get the attention you require. Especially effective when combined with the Sniff. See below.

Holes. The Earth is overheating and needs aerating. So do your part by digging as many of these as you can.

Housebreaking. An activity that is very important to humans, so break as much of the house as possible.

Lean. Every good dog's response to the command "Sit!"—especially if your person is dressed for an evening out. Incredibly effective before black-tie events.

Leash. A strap that attaches to your collar, enabling you to lead your humans where you want them to go. Make sure that you are waiting patiently with leash in mouth when your owner comes home from work. This immediately makes your owner feel guilty, and the walk is lengthened by a good ten minutes.

Love. A feeling of intense affection, given freely and without restriction. The best way you can show your love is to wag your tail. If you're lucky, a human will love you in return, even if humans don't wag.

Sniff. A social custom to use when you greet other dogs or those people who sometimes smell like dogs.

Sofa. An object that is to dogs as napkins are to humans. After eating, it is polite to run up and down the front of the sofa and wipe your whiskers clean.

Tail. A welcome waggin'. The part of a dog's body they wear their heart on. A disadvantage to the canine poker player because every time you're dealt a good hand, you wag it.

Thunder. A signal that the world is coming to an end. Humans remain amazingly calm during thunderstorms, so it is necessary to warn them of the danger by trembling uncontrollably, rolling your eyes wildly, and panting at their heels.

Toilet. Punch bowl. Humans wonder why dogs always drink out of their toilets, but look at it from a dog's point of view: Why do humans keep peeing into our punch bowls?

Tongue. The seat of a dog's pants.

Vacuum Cleaner. Nature abhors a vacuum, and so do you.

Wastebasket. A dog toy filled with paper, envelopes, and old candy wrappers. When you get bored, turn over the basket and strew the papers all over the house until your human comes home. This is particularly fun to do when there are guests for dinner and you prance around with the contents of that very special bathroom wastepaper basket.

Yummy. Anything on a human's plate.

First Dogs 9

> You want a friend
> in Washington?
> Get a dog.
> —*Harry Truman*

Many of our American presidents have been top dogs—*Thomas Jeffurson, Androol Jackson* and *Androol Johnson, William Henry* and *Benjamin Hairyson, Zachary Tailer, Abraham Lickin', Ulysses Pant, Rufferford Hayes, James Arfield, Chester Arfer, Rover Cleveland, William McKinleash, Fleadore Roosevelt, William Bow-Wow-ard Taft, Calvin Droolidge, Harry True to Man, Bite Eisenhowler, John F. Kenneldy, Richard Nips'em, George H.W.* and *George W. Bushy-tail,* and *Bark Obama,* who defeated *John McCainine.*

No surprise then that almost all presidents of the United States have had pets, and most of them have been dogs:

- George Washington owned thirty-six foxhounds, with inventive names such as Chaunter, Mopsy, Truelove, Sweetlips, and Vulcan.

- The largest and the smallest dogs to live in the White House were both there during the tenure of President James Buchanan. The president owned a Newfoundland named Lara. His niece, Harriet Lane, who served as White House hostess because the president was unmarried, had a tiny toy terrier named Punch.

- Among the six dogs that Theodore Roosevelt owned during his presidency was a bull terrier named Pete, who ripped off a French ambassador's pants in the White House.

- Warren Harding's Airedale, Laddie Boy, was assigned a valet and occupied a handcarved chair at cabinet meetings.

- Franklin Roosevelt's beloved Scottie, Fala, had a press secretary, starred in a movie, and was named an honorary private in the army. Roosevelt responded to a political rumor that he had abused his office by sending a U.S. Navy destroyer to pick up Fala in the Aleutian Islands:

  Republican leaders have not been content with attacks on me, or my wife, or my sons. No, not content with that, they now include my little dog, Fala. Well, of course, I don't resent attacks, and my family doesn't resent attacks, but Fala *does* resent them. You know, Fala is Scotch, and being a Scottie, as soon as he learned that the Republican fiction writers in Congress and out had concocted a story that I had left him behind on the Aleutian Islands and had sent a destroyer back to find him—at a cost to the taxpayers of two or three, or eight or twenty million dollars—his Scotch soul was furious. He has not been the same dog since!

- During the 1952 presidential campaign, Richard Nixon, the Republican candidate for vice president, was accused of using a slush fund of political contributions for his personal whims. In a clever half-hour rebuttal that appears to be influenced by Roosevelt's earlier explanation, Nixon revealed that he had received—and kept—a gift from one political supporter. Nixon's performance quickly became known as the Checkers speech:

  A man down in Texas heard Pat on the radio mention the fact that our two youngsters would like to have a dog. And, believe it or not, the day before we left on this campaign trip we got a message from

Union Station in Baltimore saying they had a package for us. We went down to get it. You know what it was? It was a little cocker spaniel in a crate that he'd sent all the way from Texas, black and white, spotted. And our little girl Tricia, the six year old, named it "Checkers." And you know, the kids, like all kids, love the dog, and I just want to say this right now, that regardless of what they say about it, we're gonna keep it.

- Lyndon Johnson had two beagles named Him and Her. The president caught considerable flack for picking up Him by the ears. The White House was deluged by calls from angry dog lovers.

- Ronald Reagan's King Charles spaniel, Rex, often dragged his master and mistress away from reporters and photographers by pulling hard on his leash.

- Barbara Bush wrote *Millie's Book* about her English springer spaniel, the most popular First Dog in history. Millie's "autobiography" was on the best-seller list for twenty-nine weeks and sold more copies than the president's life story.

10 A Dozen Distinguished Dogs

My little dog—a heartbeat at my feet.
—*Edith Wharton*

Many famous dogs, both real and imaginary, have made their mark outside the White House:

LASSIE

1. In ancient Greek mythology, Cerberus was the three-headed dog that guarded the underworld. He had a snake for a tail and snakes down his back like a mane. The last of the twelve labors of the Greek hero Hercules was to capture this "Hound of Hades" and deliver him to the Mycenaean king, Eurystheus. After completing that task, Hercules returned Cerberus unharmed to the underworld.

2. In Homer's *Odyssey*, Odysseus's dog Argos is the only one who recognizes the Greek hero when, after twenty years away, he returns home disguised as a beggar. When he sees Argos, Odysseus sheds a tear but makes sure that no one notices. "But Argos passed into the darkness of death, now that he had seen his master once more after twenty years."

3. On the grave behind an iron fence in the town of Beddgelert, North Wales, stands a marker that recounts the legend of Gelert, a hound owned by the thirteenth-century prince Llewelyn. One day Gelert disappeared mysteriously as his master rode out to the hunt. When the prince returned, his infant son was nowhere to be found. The child's crib was overturned and bloody, and Gelert's fangs were dripping with blood.

   Convinced that the dog had savaged the baby, Prince Llewelyn drew his sword and plunged it into the dog. Gelert's dying cry awoke the sleeping child, who was concealed under the bedding. Hidden under the bed was the body of an enormous wolf, with its throat torn out.

Overcome with remorse, Llewelyn buried the dog with great ceremony. But the prince was ever after haunted by the dying yelp, and he never smiled again.

4. Nipper was once recognized by millions of music lovers. The record label for HMV ("His Master's Voice") featured a picture of Nipper listening to his master's gramophone.

5. Bingo is the name of the dog on the Cracker Jack box. The boy on the box is Sailor Jack. The pair is modeled on F. W. Rueckheim's grandson, Robert, and his dog. Rueckheim was the inventor of Cracker Jack.

6. In 1957, the dog Laika became the first living being in space via an earth satellite. John F. Kennedy's terrier Charlie fathered four puppies with Laika's daughter.

7. Rin Tin Tin was the first Hollywood dog star. He signed his movie contracts—all twenty-six of them—with a pawprint. The early canine stars in Hollywood, including Rin Tin Tin, Rusty, and Strongheart, were German shepherds. In those innocent days, German shepherds also played the part of wolves. The dog stars Rin Tin Tin, Strongheart, and Lassie are the only three animals who have stars on the Hollywood Walk of Fame.

8. Toto, in *The Wizard of Oz*, was played by a female cairn terrier named Terry. She was already a star of some magnitude and was chosen from hundreds of tests and photographs submitted to the studio for the part of Toto.

9. The fictional dog Lassie was created by Eric Mowbray Knight in the short novel "Lassie Come-Home." The dog in the story was based on Knight's real-life collie, Toots. All collies playing the female Lassie in the movies have been male. Male collies are larger than female collies and tend to look better on camera. The male's size allows a child actor to play opposite the dog for longer before outgrowing him.

10. Old Yeller was the dog in popular books by Fred Gipson and subsequent films. Gipson explains the double meaning of the dog's name: "One part meant that his short hair was a dingy yellow, a color that we called 'yeller' in those days. The other meant that when he opened his mouth, the sound he let out was closer to a yell than a bark."

11. George Lucas's Alaskan malamute, Indiana, inspired him to create the hairy Wookiee Chewbacca in his early *Star Wars* films.

12. Finally, there's Fluffy, the three-headed dog who guarded the Philosopher's Stone at Hogwarts School of Witchcraft and Wizardry. Harry Potter, Ron Weasley, and Hermione Granger will never forget Fluffy.

Cartoon Dogs 11

Happiness is a warm puppy.
—*Charles M. Schulz*

For a century, dogs have ambled, trotted, scampered, and barked through our comic strips. Occasionally a strip is named after the dog itself, as in *Fred Basset, Howard Huge,* and *Marmaduke.* In other funnies, the dog is simply one player in a pen-and-ink cast. Match each dog in the left-paw column with its comic strip home in the right-paw column. Answers follow.

1. Barfy	*Beetle Bailey*
2. Daisy	*Blondie*
3. Dogbert	*Bloom County*
4. Earl	*Cathy*
5. Electra	*Dennis the Menace*
6. Odie	*Dilbert*
7. Otto	*The Family Circus*
8. Poncho	*Garfield*

9. Roscoe	*Get Fuzzy*
10. Rosebud	*Hagar the Horrible*
11. Ruff	*Little Orphan Annie*
12. Sandy	*Mutts*
13. Satchel Pooch	*Peanuts*
14. Snert	*Pickles*
15. Snoopy	*Pooch Café*

Answers

1. *The Family Circus* 2. *Blondie* 3. *Dilbert* 4. *Mutts* 5. *Cathy* 6. *Garfield* 7. *Beetle Bailey* 8. *Pooch Café* 9. *Pickles* 10. *Bloom County* 11. *Dennis the Menace* 12. *Little Orphan Annie* 13. *Get Fuzzy* 14. *Hagar the Horrible* 15. *Peanuts*

The Creation of Dogs and Cats **12**

God . . . sat down for a moment when the dog was finished
in order to watch it . . . and to know that it was good,
that nothing was lacking,
that it could not have been made better.

—*Rainer Maria Rilke*

And Adam said, "Lord, when I was in the garden, You walked with me every day. Now I do not see You anymore. I am lonesome here and it is difficult for me to remember how much You love me."

And God said, "No problem! I will create a companion for you who will be with you forever and who will be a reflection of My love for you, so that you will know I love you, even when you cannot see Me. Regardless of how selfish and childish and unlovable you may be, this new companion will accept you as you are and will love you as I do, in spite of yourself."

And God created a new animal to be a companion for Adam. And it was a good creature. And God was pleased.

And the new animal was pleased to be with Adam and he wagged his tail. And Adam said, "But Lord, I have already named all the animals in the Kingdom and all the good names are taken and I cannot think of a name for this new animal."

And God said, "No problem! Because I have created this new animal to be a reflection of my love for you, his name will be a reflection of my own name, and you will call him DOG."

And Dog lived with Adam and was a companion to him and loved him. And Adam was comforted. And God was pleased. And Dog was content and wagged his tail.

After a while, it came to pass that Adam's guardian angel came to the Lord and said, "Lord, Adam has become filled with pride. He struts and preens like a peacock, and he believes he is worthy of adoration. Dog has indeed taught him that he is loved, but no one has taught him humility."

And the Lord said, "No problem! I will create for him a companion who will be with him forever and who will see him as he is. The companion will remind him of his limitations, so he will know that he is not worthy of adoration."

And God created Cat to be a companion to Adam. And Cat would not obey Adam.

And when Adam gazed into Cat's eyes, he was reminded that he was not the supreme being. And Adam learned humility.

And God was pleased. And Adam was greatly improved.

And Cat did not care one way or the other.

How the Dog Got Its Name

When God had made the earth and sky
The flowers and the trees,
He then made all the animals,
The fish, the birds, and bees.

And when at last He'd finished,
Not one was quite the same.
He said, "I'll walk this world of mine
And give each one a name."

And so He traveled far and wide;
And everywhere He went,
A little creature followed Him
Until its strength was spent.

When all were named upon the earth
And in the sky and sea,
The little creature said, "Dear Lord,
There's not one left for me."

Kindly the Father said to him,
"I've left you to the end.
I've turned my own name back to front
And called you 'dog,' my friend."

13 Ten Commandments for Dog Owners

Dog ownership is
like a rainbow.
Puppies are the joy
at one end.
Old dogs are the treasure
at the other.

—*Carolyn Alexander*

I. Thou shalt remember that my life is likely to last ten to fifteen years. Any separation from you will be painful for me. Remember that before you adopt me.

II. Thou shalt give me time to understand what you want of me. Treat me kindly, my beloved friend, for no heart in all the world is more grateful for kindness than this loving heart of mine.

III. Thou shalt place your trust in me. It is crucial to my well being.

IV. Thou shalt not be angry with me for long and shalt not lock me up as punishment. You have your work, your entertainment, and your friends. I have only you.

V. Thou shalt be aware that no matter how you treat me, I'll never forget it.

VI. Thou shalt talk to me sometimes. Even if I don't understand your words, I understand your voice when it's speaking to me. Speak to me often, for your voice is the world's sweetest music, as you must know by the fierce wagging of my tail whenever you greet me.

VII. Before hitting me, thou shalt remember that I have teeth that could easily crush the bones in your hand, but I choose not to bite you. Before beating me, know that patience and understanding will more quickly teach me the things you would have me learn.

VIII. Before scolding me for being lazy or contrary, thou shalt ask thyself if something might be bothering me. Perhaps I am not getting the right food or I've been out in the sun too long or my heart is growing old and weak.

IX. Thou shalt take care of me when I get old. You, too, will grow old one day.

X. When the time comes for my final journey, thou shalt see that my trusting life is taken gently. I shall leave this earth knowing with the last breath I draw that you have loved me till the end. That is only fitting because you know how much I love you.

14 Our Sacred Pets

Until one has loved an animal,
a part of one's soul remains unawakened.

—*Anatole France*

A Prayer for Animals

Hear our humble prayer, O God, for our friends the animals, especially for animals who are suffering; for any that are hunted or lost or deserted or frightened or hungry; for all that must be put to death.

We entreat for them all Thy mercy and pity, and for those who deal with them we ask a heart of compassion and gentle hands and kindly words.

Make us, ourselves, to be true friends to animals and so to share the blessings of the merciful.

—*Albert Schweitzer*

A Dog's Best Friend

O Lord, don't let me once forget
How I love my trusty pet.
Help me learn to disregard
Canine craters in my yard.

Show me how to be a buddy
Even when my sofa's muddy.
Don't allow my pooch to munch
Postal carriers for lunch,

Shield my neighbor's cat from view.
Guide my steps around the doo.
Train me not to curse and scowl
When it's puppy's night to howl.

Grant I shan't awake in fear
With a cold nose in my ear.
Give me patience without end.
Help me be my dog's best friend.

A Dog's Soul

Every dog must have a soul
Somewhere deep inside,
Where all his hurts and grievances
Are buried with his pride,
Where he decides the good and bad,
The wrong way from the right,
And where his judgment carefully
Is hidden from our sight.

A dog must have a secret place
Where every thought abides,
A sort of close acquaintance that
He trusts in and confides.
And when accused unjustly for
Himself, he cannot speak,
Rebuked, he finds within his soul
The comfort he must seek.

He'll love, though he is unloved,
And he'll serve though badly used,
And one kind word will wipe away
The times when he's abused.
Although his heart may break in two,
His love will still be whole,
Because God gave to every dog
An understanding soul.

All Dogs Go to Heaven 15

If there are no dogs in Heaven,
then when I die, I want to go
where they went.

—*Will Rogers*

A Man and His Dog

A man and his dog were walking along a road. The man was enjoying the walk, when it suddenly occurred to him that he was dead. He remembered dying, and that his dog had been dead for years. He wondered where the road was leading them.

After a while, they came to a high, white stone wall along one side of the road. It looked like fine marble. The man and his dog walked toward the gate, and as he got closer, he saw a man at a desk to one side. When he was close enough, he called out, "Excuse me, where are we?"

"This is Heaven, sir," the man at the desk answered.

"Wow! Would you happen to have some water?" the man asked.

"Of course, sir. Come right in, and I'll have some ice water brought right up." The man gestured, and the gate began to open.

"May my friend come in, too?" the traveler asked, gesturing toward his dog.

"I'm sorry, sir, but we don't accept pets."

The man thought a moment and then turned back toward the road and continued the way he had been going. After another long walk, and at the top of another long hill, he came to a dirt road that led through a farm gate that looked as if it had never been closed. There was no fence. As he approached the gate, he saw a man inside, leaning against a tree and reading a book.

"Excuse me," he called to the reader. "Do you have any water?"

"Sure, there's a pump over there." The man with the book pointed to a place that couldn't be seen from outside the gate. "Come on in."

"How about my friend here?" The traveler gestured to his dog.

"There should be a bowl by the pump."

They went through the gate, and sure enough, there was an old-fashioned hand pump with a bowl beside it. The traveler filled the bowl and took a long drink himself. Then he gave some to his dog. When they were full, he and the dog walked back toward the man, who was standing by the tree waiting for them.

"What do you call this place?" the traveler asked.

"This is Heaven," came the answer.

"Well, that's confusing," the traveler said. "The man down the road said that was Heaven, too."

"Oh, you mean the place with the gold street and gleaming gate? Nope, that's Hell."

"Doesn't it make you mad for them to use your name like that?"

"No. I can see how you might think so, but we're just happy that they screen out the folks who'd leave their best friends behind."

Treasured Friend

I lost a treasured friend today—
The little dog who used to lay
Her gentle head upon my knee
And share her silent thoughts with me.

She'll come no longer to my call,
Retrieve no more her favorite ball.
A voice far greater than my own
Has called her to His golden throne.

Although my eyes are filled with tears,
I thank Him for the happy years
He let her spend down here with me
And for her love and loyalty.

When it is time for me to go
And join her there, this much I know:
I shall not fear the transient dark,
For she will greet me with her bark.

16 Dogs' Letters to God

St. Peter: "The Pearly Gates
are no big deal.
It only became heaven after we added
the doggy door."
—*Vic Lee,* Pardon My Planet

- *Dear God:* Why do humans smell the flowers, but seldom, if ever, smell one another?

- *Dear God:* When we get to Heaven, can we sit on your couch? Or is it going to be the same old story?

- *Dear God:* Are there dogs on other planets or are we alone? I have been howling at the moon and stars for a long time, but all I ever hear back is the collie across the street.

- *Dear God:* Why are there cars named after the jaguar, the cougar, the mustang, the colt, the stingray, and the rabbit, but not *one* named for a dog? How often do you see a cougar riding around? We dogs love a nice ride. Would it be so hard to rename the Chrysler Eagle the Chrysler Beagle?

- *Dear God:* If we come back as humans, is that good or bad?

- *Dear God:* If a dog barks his head off in the forest and no human hears him, is he still a bad dog?

- *Dear God:* We dogs can understand human verbal instructions, hand signals, whistles, horns, clickers, beepers, scent IDs, electromagnetic energy fields, and Frisbee flight paths. What do humans understand?

- *Dear God:* More meatballs, less spaghetti, please.

50

- *Dear God:* When we get to the Pearly Gates, do we have to shake hands to get in?

- *Dear God:* Are there mailmen in Heaven? If there are, will I have to apologize?

- And, Master, here is my last question: When I get to Heaven, can you undo what that veterinarian did to me?

17 A Dog's Night Before Christmas

(with thanks to Clement Clarke Moore)

'Twas the night before Christmas, and all through the house
Not a creature was stirring, not even a mouse.
The stockings were hung by the chimney with care
In hopes that Saint Nicholas soon would be there.

My dogs, they were nestled all snug in their beds,
While visions of chewy toys danced in their heads.
When up on the roof there arose such a clatter,
I sprang from my chair to see what was the matter.

Off to the window I flew like a flash,
Tore open the shutter, then threw up the sash.
The moon on the crest of the new-fallen snow
Gave a luster of midday to objects below.

And what to my wondering eyes should appear
But a miniature sleigh and eight tiny reindeer.
With a little old driver so lively and quick,
I knew in a moment it must be St. Nick.

With a sputter of ashes and flurry of soot,
He slid down the chimney with all of his loot.
My precious dogs stood there, so regal and proud,
Guarding our home with their barks oh so loud.

St. Nick showed no fear, and he called them by name.
He knew in his heart they were gentle and tame.
He brought out his list, began checking it twice.
"My beauties, I see that all year you've been nice.

"I have in my bag many toys and much more.
Please tell me, you puppies, what you're longing for."
My dogs talked to each other—much to my surprise
And then turned to Santa with tears in their eyes.

"We have chewies and balls and ropes to be tugged.
We are pampered and coddled and petted and hugged.
But for Christmas, dear Santa, we have but one care:
That all dogs be loved just as much as we are.

"We want no dog beaten, no dog whipped or chained.
We want no dog abused, abandoned, or maimed.
We want that all dogs, no matter what size,
See true love reflected in their masters' eyes."

St. Nick paused for a moment to gather his wits.
"I cannot stop humans from being such twits.
All dogs are so beautiful and such a treasure.
They just want to be loved and to give humans pleasure.

"This is a bright lesson I will try to teach.
And maybe your wish will be within my reach."
St. Nick then turned to me, his face wet with tears:
"Be proud of your babies. They all are such dears."

He planted a kiss on each beautiful head:
"Now you gentle giants, go right off to bed.
Think only good thoughts, and dream only good dreams
Of running and jumping and playing in streams."

In an instant, St. Nick disappeared in a poof,
And I heard him laugh loudly up there on the roof.
He jumped in his sleigh, to his team gave a whistle,
And away they all flew like the down of a thistle.

But I heard him exclaim, ere he drove out of sight,
"Merry Christmas to All, and to Dogs a Good Life!"

A Dog's New Year's Resolutions 18

A dog reflects family life.
Whoever saw a frisky dog
in a gloomy family,
or a sad dog
in a happy one?
—*Arthur Conan Doyle*

- I will not use the sofa or Mom's and Dad's laps as a face towel.

- I will remember that the garbage collector is not stealing our stuff.

- I will learn that my head does not belong in the refrigerator.

- I will not bite the officer's hand when he reaches in for Mom's driver's license and registration.

- I will not play tug-of-war with Dad's underwear when he's on the toilet.

- I will not steal Mom's underwear and dance all over the backyard with it.

- I do not need to suddenly stand straight up when I'm lying under the coffee table.

- I will shake the rainwater out of my fur before entering the house.

- I will not throw up in the car.

- When out for a walk, I will not leave mementos on the neighbors' lawns.
- At the dog park I will stop downloading as far away as possible from my master.
- I will not roll on dead seagulls, fish, crabs, or poop just because I like the way they smell.
- I will not eat the cats' food before they eat it or after they throw it up.
- I will not wake Mom and Dad up by sticking my cold, wet nose against them.
- I will not wake Mom and Dad by barking in the middle of the night, even though I know they are reassured by my efforts to protect the house.
- I will not lick my humans' toothbrush and not tell them.
- When in the car, I will not insist on having the window rolled down when it's freezing or raining outside.
- I will strive to remember that we do not have a doorbell, so I won't bark each time I hear one on TV.
- I will remember that the cat is not a squeaky toy—so when I play with him and he makes that noise, it's usually not a good thing.

You call to a dog and a dog will break its neck to get to you.
Dogs just want to please.
Call to a cat and its attitude is "What's in it for me?"

—Lewis Grizzard

Dogs lick you because they love you.
Cats lick you because you had chicken for dinner.
If a dog jumps up into your lap,
it is because he is fond of you;
but if a cat does the same thing,
it is because your lap is warmer.

—Alfred North Whitehead

I've been trying to train my cat
to understand the meaning of the word "no."
Which seems to be equivalent to teaching a dog Latin.

—Judy Brown

Women and cats will do as they please,
and men and dogs should relax and get used to the idea.
—*Robert Heinlein*

In order to keep a true perspective of one's importance,
everyone should have a dog that will worship him
and a cat that will ignore him.
—*Dereke Bruce*

To someone very good and just,
　Who has proved worthy of her trust,
The cat will sometimes condescend—
　The dog is everybody's friend.
　　　—*Oliver Hereford*

The humble dog don't ask for much—
　A praiseful word, a bone, and such.
He's grateful for the passing touch
　And loves those who bestow it.

The lofty cat struts, nose in air.
　You call; it answers with a stare,
Accepts, demands the finest care,
　Then acts as if you owe it.
　　　—*Benjamin Franklin Pierce*

A dog lives in your house and sees that you give it food and water and says to itself, "Wow, these beings give me food and water without my having to do anything. They must be gods!"

A cat lives in your house and sees that you give it food and water and says to herself, "Wow, these beings give me food and water without my having to do anything. I must be a god!"

A dog sees its master trapped on the roof of the house and thinks, "Yikes! My master is in trouble!" A cat sees its master trapped on the roof of the house and thinks, "Yikes! I don't know how to use a can opener!"

If you command your dog to "Come here," he runs right over with a "Yes, what can I do for you?" The cat's response is "Put it in writing, and I'll get back to you later." This is why dogs have masters, and cats have staff.

What Is a Cat?

- Cats do what they want.
- They rarely listen to you.
- They are totally unpredictable.
- When you want to play, they want to be alone.
- When you want to be alone, they want to play.
- They expect you to cater to their every whim.
- They are moody.
- They leave hair everywhere.
- They are slinky.
- They purr when they are happy.

- They are finicky about their food.
- They scratch when they are angry.
- They do not understand what you see in dogs.
- *Conclusion:* Cats are furry little women.

What Is a Dog?

- Dogs spend all day sprawled on the most comfortable piece of furniture in the house.
- They take up too much room in the bed.
- They can hear a package of food opening half a block away, but don't hear you when you're in the same room.
- They can look dumb and lovable all at the same time.
- They growl when they are not happy.
- When you want to play, they want to play.
- When you want to be alone, they want to play.
- They leave their toys everywhere.
- They do disgusting things with their mouths and then try to give you a kiss.
- They have an irrational fear of vacuum cleaners.
- They don't tell you what's bothering them.
- They mark their territory.
- They don't do dishes.

- They like to play dominance games.
- They don't notice when you get your hair cut.
- They do not understand what you see in cats.
- *Conclusion:* Dogs are furry little men.

Why Dogs Are Better Than Cats

- Cats poop in your house every day. Dogs wouldn't be caught dead or alive doing that.
- When a dog wags his tail, he's happy. When a cat wags her tail, she's perturbed, as usual.
- Dogs will tilt their heads and try to understand every word you say. Cats will ignore you and take a nap.
- Dogs will let you give them a bath without taking out a contract on your life.
- Cats look silly on a leash and even sillier hauling a sled.
- When you come home from work, your dog will be happy and lick your face. Cats will still be mad at you for leaving in the first place.
- Dogs will give you unconditional love until the day they die. Cats will make you pay for every mistake you've ever made since the day you were born.
- A dog knows when you're sad, and he'll try to comfort you. Cats don't care how you feel, as long as you remember where the can opener is.
- Dogs will bring you your slippers. Cats will drop a dead mouse in your slippers.

- Give a dog a toy, and he will play with it for hours. Give a cat a toy, and she will play with the wrapper for ten minutes.

- When you take them for a ride, dogs will sit on the seat next to you. Cats have to have their own private basket, or they won't go at all.

- Dogs will come when you call them, and they'll be happy. Cats will have someone take a message and get back to you.

- Dogs will play fetch with you all day long. The only things cats will play with all day long are small rodents or bugs.

- Dogs will wake you up if the house is on fire. Cats will quietly sneak out the back door.

A Tail of Two Diaries 20

A dog is a man's
best friend.
A cat is a cat's best friend.
—*Robert J. Vogel*

Excerpt from a Dog's Diary

Day 1,054

8:00 A.M.—Woke up and stretched! *My favorite thing!*

8:30 A.M.—Dog food! *My favorite thing!*

9:30 A.M.—A car ride! *My favorite thing!*

9:40 A.M.—A walk in the park! *My favorite thing!*

10:30 A.M.—Got rubbed and petted! *My favorite thing!*

12:00 noon—Lunch! *My favorite thing!*

1:00 P.M.—The yard! *My favorite thing!*

2:30 P.M.—Eww. A bath. Bummer.

3:00 P.M.—Milk bones! *My favorite thing!*

4:00 P.M.—The kids! *My favorite thing!*

5:00 P.M.—Got to play ball! *My favorite thing!*

6:00 P.M.—Pooped in the yard! *My favorite thing!*

7:00 P.M.—Watched TV with the family! *My favorite thing!*

10:00 P.M.—Snack! *My favorite thing!*

10:30 P.M.—Slept on the bed! *My favorite thing!*

Chapter 20

Excerpt from a Cat's Diary

Day 1,054

My captors continue to taunt me with bizarre little dangling objects. They dine lavishly on fresh meat, while I am forced to eat dry nuggets. Although I make my contempt for the rations perfectly clear, I still must consume something to keep up my strength. The only thing that keeps me going is my hope of escape, and the mild satisfaction I get from destroying drapes and scratching furniture. Tomorrow I may eat another houseplant.

Day 1,055

Today I was almost successful in my attempt to assassinate one of my captors by weaving around their feet while they were walking. I must try this at the top of the stairs. In an attempt to disgust and repulse these vile oppressors, I once again induced myself to throw up on their favorite chair. I must try this upon their bed.

Day 1,056

I have decapitated a mouse and brought them the headless body, in an attempt to make them aware of what I am capable of, and to try to strike fear into their hearts. They only cooed and condescended about "what a good little hunter" I was. Hmmm. Not working according to plan.

Over time, I have come to see how sadistic they are. This afternoon, for no good reason, I was chosen for the water torture. This time it included a burning foamy chemical called "shampoo." What sick minds could invent such a liquid. My only consolation is the piece of thumb still stuck between my teeth.

Day 1,057

There was some sort of gathering of their accomplices. I was placed in solitary throughout the event. However, I could hear the noise and smell the foul odor of the glass tubes they call "beer." I overheard that my confinement was due to my power of "allergies." Must learn what this is and how to use it to my advantage.

I am convinced the other captives are flunkies and snitches. The dog is routinely released and seems more than happy to return. He is obviously a half-wit. The bird, on the other hand, must be an informant, and speaks with them regularly. I am certain he reports my every move. My captors have arranged protective custody for him in an elevated metal cell. He is safe—for now.

21 The Difference Between Dogs and People

The better I get to know men,
the more I find myself loving dogs.
—*Charles De Gaulle*

Why a Dog Is Better Than a Woman

- A dog's parents never visit.

- A dog loves you when you leave your clothes or anything else on the floor.

- A dog limits its time in the bathroom to a quick drink.

- A dog never expects you to telephone.

- A dog will not get mad at you if you forget its birthday.

- A dog never expects flowers on Valentine's Day.

- A dog does not care about the previous dogs in your life.

- A dog does not get mad at you if you play with another dog.

- The later you are, the happier a dog is to see you.

- Dogs don't cry.
- You can buy a dog's affection with a squeaky toy.
- Dogs love it when your friends come over.
- Dogs don't care if you use their shampoo.
- Dogs think you sing great.
- Dogs don't notice if you call them by another dog's name.
- Dogs are excited by rough play.
- Dogs understand that flatulence is funny.
- Dogs love red meat.
- Dogs can appreciate excessive body hair.
- If a dog is gorgeous, other dogs don't hate it.
- A dog's disposition stays the same all month long.
- Dogs never need to examine the relationship.
- Dogs love long car trips.
- Dogs understand that instincts are better than asking for directions.
- Dogs like beer.
- Dogs don't hate their bodies.
- Dogs don't whine as much.
- No dog ever put on a hundred pounds after reaching adulthood.
- Dogs agree that you have to raise your voice to get your point across.
- Dogs don't let magazine articles guide their lives.
- Dogs would rather have you buy them a hamburger than a lobster dinner.

- Dogs never want foot rubs.
- Dogs enjoy heavy petting in public.
- Dogs find you amusing when you're drunk.
- Dogs can't talk.
- Dogs aren't catty.
- Dogs seldom outlive you.
- Dogs don't shop.

Why a Dog Is Better Than a Man

- You can find a nice dog by advertising on a card in a shop window or in the classified section of the local paper.
- Dogs have no trouble expressing their feelings in public.
- Dogs miss you when you are gone.
- Dogs feel guilty when they do something wrong.
- Dogs don't brag about past relationships.
- Dogs don't criticize your friends.
- Dogs are very direct about wanting to go out.
- Dogs are already in touch with their inner puppies.
- Dogs can be house-trained.
- Dogs roll over and play dead to impress you. A man will roll over and play dead only if you ask him to get up and make coffee.
- Dogs are less careless about leaving puddles on the bathroom floor.

- Dogs will bring you the newspaper without first tearing it apart to remove the sports section.
- Dogs will never touch the remote, don't care about football, and will cuddle up next to you as you watch romantic movies.
- Middle-aged dogs seldom leave you for a younger owner.
- Dogs mean it when they kiss you.
- Dogs don't care whether or not you shave your legs.
- Dogs don't mind if you do all the driving.
- Dogs obsess about you as much as you obsess about them.
- Dogs don't play games with you—except fetch (and then they don't laugh at how you throw).
- Dogs don't feel threatened by female intelligence.
- You don't have to worry about who your dog is dreaming about.
- Good-looking dogs don't know they are good looking.
- Dogs understand what the word *no* means.
- Dogs love to go for long walks in the woods.
- Dogs don't want to bring their friends home for a beer.
- Dogs don't tell the punch lines to your jokes.
- When dogs beg, it's cute. When men beg, it's pathetic.
- Dogs admit when they are jealous.
- Dogs admit it when they are lost.
- Dogs don't care if you have lipstick on when you kiss them.

- Dogs don't mind morning breath.
- Dogs love you without your morning shower and all the foo foo stuff.
- Dogs are satisfied with a belly rub.
- Dogs don't complain about the amount of money you spend on clothes.
- Dogs are faithful.
- Dogs are better protection against intruders.
- "Work like a dog" is strenuous. "Work like a man" is, uhm—not.
- Dogs can be neutered legally.
- Dogs are willing to make fools of themselves simply over the joy of seeing you.
- Dogs are content to get up on your bed just to warm your feet, and you can push them off when they snore.
- Dogs don't nag or manipulate with guilt trips.
- Dogs know exactly what you need when you are sick.
- Dogs won't work your crossword in ink.
- Dogs never answer your phone or borrow your car.
- Dogs don't turn your bathroom into a library.
- Dogs don't go through your medicine chest.
- Dogs don't use your toothbrush, roll-on, or hairspray.
- Dogs leave the toilet seat the way you left it.
- Dogs don't compare you to a centerfold.
- Dogs will never call and say, "I have to work late, honey."

- Dogs never have midlife crises.
- Dogs don't get embarrassed when you call them by a pet name when their friends are around.
- Dogs don't have softball practice on the day you move.
- Dogs don't care if you make more money than they do.
- Dogs don't ask to be put through medical school.
- Dogs whine less.
- There are fewer reasons to muzzle a dog in public.
- Dogs sometimes dig in the garden.
- Most dogs are really good with children.
- Dogs are far less irritating when they sit in the back of a car.
- A dog will eat whatever you put in front of him and never tell you that it's not as good as his mother's cooking.
- Dogs are always willing to go out, at any hour, for as long and wherever you want.
- Dogs have a highly developed sense of smell. Men, on the other hand, can quite happily wear the same pair of pants for a week.
- You'd feel guilty about turning a dog out on the street.
- Dogs never criticize what you do, don't care if you are pretty or ugly, fat or thin, young or old. Dogs act as if every word you say is especially worthy of listening to, and they love you unconditionally and perpetually.

On the other hand and paw, if you want someone who will never come when you call, ignores you totally when you come home, leaves hair all over the place, walks all over you, runs around all night and comes back only to eat and sleep, and acts as if your entire existence is solely to ensure his happiness, . . .

. . . then buy a cat.

Why Dogs Might Be Better Than Kids

It's been said that "Children are for people who can't have dogs." That may be going a bit far. I am the father of three children, and I do love them as much as I love my dogs. Still, here's Why Dogs Are Better Than Kids:

- Dogs eat less.
- Dogs don't ask for money all the time.
- Dogs are easier to train.
- Dogs normally come when called.
- Dogs never ask to drive the car.
- Dogs don't smoke, drink, or use drugs.
- Dogs don't have to buy the latest fashions.
- Dogs don't want to wear your clothes.
- Dogs don't need a bazillion dollars for college.
- Dogs can't see television images, so they don't grab the remote from you.

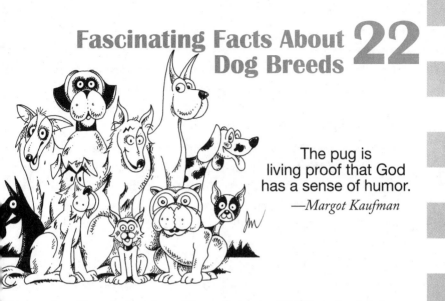

> The pug is
> living proof that God
> has a sense of humor.
> —*Margot Kaufman*

The word *pedigree* derives its pedigree from the Old French *pied de grue*, meaning "foot of the crane." Why? Because the clawlike, three-branched mark used in genealogical charts resembles the foot of the tall, leggy bird. *Pedigree* was first applied to human ancestry and later to the descent of dogs, cats, and other animals.

- The world's smartest dogs are thought to be the border collie, the poodle, and the golden retriever. In reality, there is only one smartest dog in the world—and you own it!

- French poodles did not originate in France. Poodles were originally used as hunting dogs in Europe. The dogs' thick coats were a hindrance in water and thick brush, so hunters sheared the hindquarters, with cuffs left around the ankles and hips to protect against rheumatism.

- About eight thousand years ago, ancient Egyptians raised hunting dogs they named saluki, an Arabic word that means "noble one." The saluki was the royal dog of Egypt and can be traced back to 329 B.C., making these dogs the oldest known breed. Sleek like the Greyhound, the saluki can run up to forty miles an hour, and its sharp eyes can spot animals moving miles away.

- The Labrador retriever is the favorite breed in the United States, Canada, and the United Kingdom. More than 125,000 Labs are registered here. That's almost three times the number of new registrations for the second-most popular breed, the Yorkshire terrier. Third and fourth are German shepherds and golden retrievers. These four breeds alone account for about 30 percent of all dogs registered.

- Saint Bernards have never, ever carried brandy barrels. Administering alcohol to anyone with hypothermia would precipitate a medical disaster. The popular misconception emanates from a series of paintings by Sir Edwin Landseer in the mid-1800s that depicted Saint Bernards wearing brandy casks.

- The Norwegian breed Lundehune has six toes, including two dewclaws, that help the dog to climb steep areas. Extra joints in the nape of the neck allow the animal to turn its head at a 180-degree angle, and the shoulder joints are extremely flexible. The ears possess unusual mobility and can close so that the ear canal is protected against dirt and moisture.

- Newfoundlands excel in swimming and water rescue because of their webbed feet and water-resistant coat.

- Basset hounds, on the other paw, cannot swim. The name for these short-legged hounds derives from the French *bas*, meaning "low" and –*et*, an attenuating suffix meaning, "rather." So *basset* means "rather low."

- The *grey* in *greyhound* is not the color but descends from an Old Norse word meaning "female." Greyhounds are the fastest dogs on earth, with speeds of almost forty-five miles an hour. A law in England from around the eleventh century states that "No meane person may keepe any greihounds."

- The dachshund is one of the oldest dog breeds in history, dating back to ancient Egypt. The name comes from one of its earliest uses—flushing badgers and other underground animals from their holes. In German, *dachs* means "badger" and *hund* means "hound."

- Up until the late 1800s, collies were known as Scottish sheepdogs. The collie is known for his elongated muzzle and coloration. This breed comes in both rough and smooth varieties in tricolor (black, white, and tan), blue merle, and sable and white.

- Originally the exclusive property of nobles and other of high rank, the bloodhound is so called because *blooded* means "aristocratic." Bloodhounds are prized for their ability to single out and identify a number of scents simultaneously. They can follow a trail that is as much as four days old and track a human scent for up to one hundred miles. Evidence from such tracking is admissible in American courts. Bloodhounds have starred in the movies *Cinderella* (Disney animated version), *Johnny and Clyde, Runaway Bride, Lady and the Tramp, Three on the Run,* and *The Aristocats*.

- In the film *Lady and the Tramp,* Lady is a cocker spaniel, but Walt Disney's family dog named Lady was a poodle.

- Dalmatians (avoid the spelling *dalmations*) get their name from Dalmatia, a region on the east coast of the Adriatic Sea. The distinctive spotted coat is unique to the dalmatian breed. Dalmatian puppies are born completely white.

- Every known dog breed but two has a pink tongue. The exceptions are the Chinese chow chow and the shar-pei, whose tongues are jet black or spotted with black. All dogs with black pigmentation on their tongues are at least partially chow chow or shar-pei.

- More than 2,500 years ago, Pekingese were the exclusive property of the ancient Chinese Imperial Court and guarded the emperors. Chinese royalty carried Pekingese puppies in the voluminous sleeves of their robes, and commoners had to bow to the Pekingese. The dogs also wore silk robes and had their own staffs to groom and care for them. Anyone outside the Imperial Court found with a Pekingese would be put to death.

- Lhasa apsos were originally bred as guard dogs in Lhasa, Tibet, more than two thousand years ago. The first Lhasa apsos in the United States were gifts from the thirteenth Dalai Lama in the 1930s.

- Akitas possess a double coat, with a dense straight undercoat and a thick outer coat. This coat makes the dog waterproof, as well as being well equipped for the fierce winters in northern Japan. Akitas came to the United States in 1937, when Helen Keller visited Japan and received one as a gift.

- Boxers are so named because of their manner of fighting and playing with their front paws. The boxer was originally bred in German from the English bulldog and the now extinct Bullenbeiser.

- The Chihuahua was named after the state in Mexico where they were discovered. Among the smallest of all dogs, they are also the longest lived, often surviving into their eighteenth year. Like human babies, Chihuahuas are born with a soft spot in their skull, which closes with age.

- Rottweilers are thought to descend from the dogs that guarded the camps and herds belonging to ancient Roman legions.

- After a pug saved the life of William of Orange, the breed became the official dog of his family, which ruled the Netherlands.

- A cross between the English bulldog and now-extinct English white terrier, the Boston terrier is one of the very few breeds "made in the USA."

- Because it was bred as a silent hunter and never as a guard dog, the basenji, an African wolf dog, is the only dog that cannot bark. It does, however, yelp, yodel, and even scream.

- There are only 350 Cisky terriers in the world, making them the rarest breed.

- The dingo is not native to Australia but was introduced thousands of years ago by the first immigrants.

- In 1859, the first formal dog show was held in Newcastle upon Tyne in England. The sixty dogs in the show were divided into just two categories: pointers and setters. Begun in 1877 in New York City, the Westminster Kennel Club Dog Show is, except for the Kentucky Derby, the oldest continuous sporting event in America. The winner of the 2009 Westminster Show was Stump, a Sussex spaniel. At ten years old, Stump was the oldest dog in the competition and the oldest by two years ever to win Best in Show. He came back from an apparently fatal disease that had forced him into retirement four years earlier.

23 The Little Dog Laughed

> The great pleasure of a dog is that you
> may make a fool of yourself with him
> and not only will he not scold you,
> but he will make a fool of himself too.
>
> —*Samuel Butler*

Have you ever wondered why dogs never get tired
of fetching sticks, or why, even if you've only left
the house for five minutes, your four-legged friend
always greets you as ecstatically as if you've been away for five years?

The answer is quite simple: he's suffering from senior momentitis. Indeed, your beloved Fido could probably write a whole book on the subject, if he could write that is, and if he could remember where he buried the pen.

Did you ever walk into a room and forget why you walked in? That's how dogs spend their lives. Some of us humans spend our lives collecting dog jokes. Here are the picks of the litter:

Three-Dog Night

A Doberman, a bulldog, and the Taco Bell Chihuahua were in a doggie bar having a cool one when a good-looking female Belgian Tervuren came up to them and said, "Whoever can say *liver* and *cheese* in a sentence can go out on a date with me."

So the Doberman said, "I love liver and cheese."

The Belgian said, "That's not good enough."

The bulldog said, "I hate liver and cheese." She said, "That's not creative enough."

Finally the Chihuahua said, "Liver alone. Cheese mine!"

The Audition

A man brought his dog to a talent agent. "This dog can talk," said the man. "Book him in theaters and nightclubs and he'll make us a fortune!"

"Prove to me that this is a talking dog," said the agent.

"Okay, how does sandpaper feel?" asked the man.

"Rough, rough!" answered the dog.

"And what's on top of a house?"

"Roof, roof!"

"And who was the greatest baseball player?"

"Ruth, Ruth!"

"Get outa here!" yelled the agent. "This act is a cheap trick!"

The man and his dog took the elevator down to the street, where the dog asked, "How could I have known the guy was a Red Sox fan?"

The Entrée

Two friends owned dogs, one a Doberman pinscher and the other a Chihuahua. The man with the Doberman pinscher said to the man with the Chihuahua, "Let's go over to that fancy restaurant and get something to eat."

The Chihuahua owner said, "We can't go in there. We have our dogs with us."

The owner of the Doberman pinscher said, "Just follow my lead." They walked over to the restaurant, and the fellow with the Doberman put on a pair of dark glasses and entered the restaurant.

The restaurant's maitre d' said, "Sorry, no pets allowed."

The Doberman owner replied, "You don't understand. This is my Seeing Eye dog."

"A Doberman pinscher?"

"Yes, they're using them now as Seeing Eye dogs. They're very good."

And the maitre d' immediately seated the man and his Doberman.

The owner of the Chihuahua figured, "What the heck," so he put on a pair of dark glasses and started to walk in.

The maitre d' said, "Sorry, no pets allowed."

"You don't understand. This is my Seeing Eye dog."

"A Chihuahua? That's your Seeing Eye dog?" asked the skeptical maitre d'.

And the guy exclaimed, "A Chihuahua?! You mean to tell me they gave me a Chihuahua?!"

Going Postal

A nervous postman on his first round walked up to a garden fence, next to which a large Doberman was lying on the grass. An old man was sitting on the patio. "Excuse me, sir, but does your dog bite?" the postman asked.

"No, he's never done that," the old guy said. So the postman opened the gate and went into the garden.

The dog ran over, snarling and growling, and bit the postman on his arms and legs. As the old man dragged the dog off, the postman yelled, "I thought you said your dog didn't bite!"

The old man replied, "He's not my dog."

The Clever Dog

A man followed a woman and her leashed dog out of a movie theater. He asked her, "I don't mean to bother you, but I couldn't help noticing that your dog was really into the movie. He cried at the right spots, he moved nervously in his seat at the boring parts. And he laughed like crazy at the funny parts. Didn't you find that unusual?"

"Yes," she replied, "I found it very unusual because he hated the book."

In Dog We Trust

A man wrote a letter to a small hotel in a Midwestern town he planned to visit on his vacation. He wrote, "I would very much like to bring my dog with me. He is well groomed and very well behaved. Would you be willing to permit me to keep him in my room with me at night?"

An immediate reply came from the hotel owner, who said, "I've been operating this hotel for many years. In all that time, I've never had a dog steal towels, bedclothes, silverware, or pictures off the walls. I've never had to evict a dog in the middle of the night for being drunk and disorderly. And I've never had a dog run out on a hotel bill. Yes indeed, your dog is welcome at my hotel. And, if your dog will vouch for you, you're welcome to stay here, too."

The Versatile Dog

A local business was looking for office help. They put a sign in the window, stating the following: HELP WANTED. Must be able to type, must be good with a computer and must be bilingual. We are an Equal Opportunity Employer."

A short time afterward, a dog trotted up to the window, saw the sign, and went inside. He looked at the receptionist and wagged his tail, then walked over to the sign, looked at it, and whined.

Getting the idea, the receptionist called in the office manager. The office manager looked at the dog and was surprised, to say the least. However, the dog looked determined, so he led him into the office. Inside, the dog jumped up on the chair and stared at the manager.

The manager said, "I can't hire you. The sign says you have to be able to type."

The dog jumped down, went to the typewriter, and proceeded to type out a perfect letter. He took out the page and gave it to the manager, then jumped back on the chair. The manager was stunned, but then told the dog, "The sign says you have to be good with a computer."

He jumped down again and went to the computer. The dog proceeded to demonstrate his expertise with various programs, produced a sample spreadsheet and database, and presented them to the manager. By this time the manager was totally dumbfounded. He looked at the dog and said, "I realize that you are a very intelligent dog and have some unique abilities. However, I still can't give you the job."

The dog jumped down, went to a copy of the sign, and put his paw on the sentences that told about being an Equal Opportunity Employer. The manager said, "Yes, but the sign also says that you have to be bilingual."

The dog looked him straight in the eye and said, "Meow."

Scan Scam

A man entered a doctor's office, sweating profusely, breathing heavily, and asking for help. The doctor rushed him into an examination room, looked him over, and said, "You are terribly overweight and out of shape, and you need to start on a regimen of strict diet and exercise immediately."

The man became agitated. "I'm in excellent shape, and I want a second opinion."

The doctor went into the back room and came out with a cat. He placed the cat on the man's chest. The cat started walking from head to toe poking and sniffing the patient's body, and finally looked at the doctor and meowed. The doctor said, "The cat thinks that you're grotesquely overweight, too."

The man was still unwilling to accept his condition, so the doctor returned to the back room and came back with a black Labrador. The dog sniffed the patient's body, walked from head to toe, and finally looked at the doctor and barked. The doctor said, "The Lab thinks you're flabby and overweight, too."

Finally resigned to the diagnosis, the man thanked the doctor and asked how much he owed. "Five hundred and fifty dollars," replied the doctor.

"Five hundred and fifty dollars just to tell me I'm out of shape!" exclaimed the man.

"Well," said the doctor, "I would only have charged you fifty dollars for my initial diagnosis. The additional five hundred dollars was for the PET scans—the CAT scan and Lab tests."

A Wrenching Experience

There was once a handyman who had a dog named Mace. Mace was a great dog, except he had one weird habit: He liked to eat grass—not just a little bit, but in quantities that would make a lawnmower blush. And nothing, it seemed, could cure him of it.

One day, the handyman lost his wrench in the tall grass while he was working outside. He looked and looked, but it was nowhere to be found. As it was getting dark, he gave up for the night and decided to look the next morning.

When he awoke, he went outside, and saw that his dog had eaten the grass around where he had been working, and his wrench now lay in plain sight, glinting in the sun. Going out to get his wrench, the handyman called the dog over to him and said, "A'grazing Mace, how sweet the hound that saved a wrench for me."

Instructions for Toilet Cleaning

1. Put both lids of the toilet up and add 1/8 cup of pet shampoo to the water in the bowl.

2. Pick up the cat and soothe him while you carry him toward the bathroom.

3. In one smooth movement, place the cat in the toilet and close both lids. You may need to stand on the lid.

4. The cat will self-agitate and make ample suds. Never mind the noises that come from the toilet; the cat is actually enjoying this.

5. Flush the toilet three or four times. This provides a power-wash and rinse.

6. Have someone open the front door of your home. Be sure that there are no people between the bathroom and the front door.

7. Stand behind the toilet as far as you can, and quickly lift both lids.

8. The cat will rocket out of the toilet, streak through the bathroom, and run outside, where he will dry himself off.

9. Both the commode and the cat will be sparkling clean.

10. Repeat process if necessary.

Sincerely,
The Dog

Hey Diddle Diddle, the Dog in the Riddle

24

All animals, except man,
know that the principal business of life
is to enjoy it.

—*Samuel Butler*

When does the weather go "Splash! Splash!
Meow! Woof!"?
When it's raining cats and dogs.

How do you know when it's raining cats and dogs?
When you step in a poodle.

What's even worse than raining cats and dogs?
Hailing taxicabs.

What do you say when it starts to drizzle?
"It's raining kittens and puppies."

What do cats and dogs say during the holidays?
"Have a Meowy Christmas and a Yappy New Year!"

What did one flea say to the other flea when they left the movie theater?
"Shall we walk or take the dog?"

What's the difference between a dog and a comma?
A dog has claws at the end of its paws, and a comma is a pause at the end of a clause.

What do you give a dog with a fever?
Mustard. It's the best thing for a hot dog.

What protest by a group of dogs occurred in 1773?
The Boston Flea Party.

What do you call a dog with no legs?
It doesn't matter. He won't come anyway.

Which side of a dog has the most hair?
The outside, of course.

What does a dog do on three legs that a man does on two legs and a woman does sitting down?
Shake hands, of course.

Where does a rottweiler sit in the movie theater?
Anywhere it wants to.

What did the dachshund say when she crossed the finish line first?
"I'm a wiener!"

How can you distinguish a dogwood tree from the others?
By its bark.

Where does a dog go to shop when she's lost her tail?
The retail store.

What do puppies call their mother's father?
Grandpaw.

What did the hungry dalmatian say when he had a meal?
"That hit the spots."

Why is it called a "litter" of puppies?
Because they mess up the whole house.

How do you stop a dog from smelling?
Put a clothespin on its nose.

How do you tell if it's too cold to go outside?
When your dog comes back in and his leg is still up.

What did the dog tell his friends when it saw somebody putting money into a parking meter?
"They've installed pay toilets!"

What dog will laugh at any joke?
A chi-ha-ha.

Where do the dogs go for the Macy's Thanksgiving parade?
New Yorkie.

Which foods definitely don't mix?
A hot dog and catsup.

What did the puppy say to the shoe?
"It's been nice gnawing you."

What did the dog say to the dogcatcher?
"You've caught me at a bad time."

Why are dogs such poor dancers?
They have two left feet.

How do you catch a runaway dog?
Hide behind a tree and make a noise like a bone.

What dog loves to take bubble baths?
A shampoodle.

Why didn't the dog speak to his hind foot?
Because it's not polite to talk back to your paw.

Where do Eskimos train their dogs?
In the mush room.

What did Elvis teach his dog?
To rock 'n' roll over.

What is the name of the play about Pavlov's dogs?
Bell, Bark, and Kennel.

What is a polite veterinarian?
One who has many a cur to see.

What is the difference between Santa Claus and a warm dog?
Santa Claus wears a whole suit, a dog just pants.

What dogs? These are my children—
little people with fur
who make my heart open a little wider.
—*Oprah Winfrey*

Have you heard about the dogs named Timex and Rolex? *They were watchdogs.* Have you heard about the watchdogs who kept running around in circles? *They were winding themselves up.* Just remember: To err is human, to make dog puns canine.

Here are some other dogs you may not know about. Have you heard about . . .

- the dog who went to the flea circus? *He stole the show.*

- the dog with thick fur? *In the winter, he wears his coat. In the summer, he wears his coat and pants.*

- the dog who boasted of running two miles to retrieve a stick? *Her story was too far-fetched.*

- the elderly dog? *He barked, "AARP! AARP!"*

- the dyslexic dog? *He barked, "Krab! Krab! Fur! Fur!"*

- the dog who accompanied his master to work every day into New York City? *He developed car pal tunnel syndrome.*

- the vampire dog? *She was a bloodhound.*

- the cross-eyed dog? *He kept barking up the wrong tree.*

- the psychic dog? *She was adopted from the E.S.P.C.A.*

- the stupid dog? *He chased parked cars.*
- the embarrassed dalmatian? *She was black and white and red all over.*
- the very friendly dog? *He never met a man he didn't lick.*
- the dog who limped into the old western saloon? *He said, "I'm looking for the man who shot my paw."*
- the dog who gave birth to puppies near the road? *She was ticketed for littering.*
- the dog who ate some table scraps? *He got splinters in his tongue.*
- the dog who kept chasing her own tail? *She was trying to make both ends meet.*
- the dog who chased a cat through a screen door? *They both strained themselves.*
- the Dublin dog who became a hairdresser? *She was an Irish setter.*
- the backyard dog who ran toward the fence? *Her leash expired.*
- the dog who performed as a comedian? *His name was Growlcho Barks.*
- the dog who played baseball? *She chased fowls, caught flies, and ran for home.*
- the famous dog general? *His name was Dogleash MacArffur.*
- the big-jawed dog who kept scratching his butt against the fence? *He became a bottomless pit.*
- the seeing-eye dog? *Her owner walked into a store, grabbed her by the hind legs, and swung her around. "I'm just browsing," explained the owner.*
- the talking dogs? *They had a bow-wow powwow.*
- the dog owned by a fireman? *His master kept putting him out.*

Never stand between a dog
and the hydrant.
—*John Peers*

Two Burning Questions

Why is it that when you blow in a dog's face, he gets mad at you, but when you take him for a car ride, he sticks his head out the window?

Why does Goofy stand erect and speak while Pluto remains on all fours? They're both dogs in the same comic strip.

All the News That's Fit to Fetch

A wife said to her husband one weekend morning, "We've got such a clever dog. He brings in the daily newspapers every morning."

Her husband replied, "Well, lots of dogs can do that."

The wife responded, "But we've never subscribed to any."

The Grammatical Dog

A true story: Beth, a high-school English teacher, lived with her friend Sam, an intelligent golden retriever. One day, Beth's mother was riding in the backseat of the car with Sam, who insisted on leaning on Mother. Mother told Sam to "lay down and behave." No action. Mother repeated, "Lay down, Sam." Still no response.

Beth turned and commanded, "Lie down, Sam," and down he went. He was, after all, the companion of an English teacher.

Tall Tails

I have two dogs who talk in their sleep. One day a visitor was astonished to hear one of my dogs bellow, "My name is Christopher Columbus! I am six hundred years old! I own America!" Then the other dog said, "I'm married to Nicole Kidman and have won three Oscars!"

When the visitor asked what was going on, I replied, "Don't worry about it. Just let sleeping dogs lie."

Dogs on the Spot

A nursery school teacher was delivering a station wagon full of kids home one day when a fire truck zoomed past. Sitting in the front seat of the truck was a dalmatian. The children started discussing the dog's duties.

"They use him to keep crowds back," said one child.

"No," said another, "he's just for good luck."

A third child brought the argument to a close: "They use the dogs," she said firmly, "to find the fire hydrants."

Gender Finder

A little boy was with his dad looking at a litter of puppies. Upon returning home, the little boy could not wait to tell his mother that there were two girl puppies and two boy puppies.

"How do you know?" asked his mother.

The boy replied, "Daddy picked them up and looked underneath. I think it's printed on the bottom."

Signs of the Times

On a Fence: Salesmen welcome. Dog food is expensive.
In a Veterinarian's waiting room: Be back in 5 minutes. Sit! Stay!

Smell-ivision

One dog to the other: "So you're Fido. It's nice to finally put a face to the scent."

A Shot in the Dark

First Man: I had to take my dog to the vet's to get a rabies shot.
Second Man: Was it mad?
First Man: It sure wasn't happy about it.

I'm So Afreud

A sad basset hound was relating his troubles to his friend. "I'm really depressed all the time and I think negative thoughts. I'm always bored, and I feel listless."

"Why not go see a psychiatrist?" suggested the friend.

"Well, I would," said the basset hound, "except that I'm not allowed on the couch."

A New Wrinkle

Old dog owner # 1: Is it true that after a while, we begin to look like our pets?
Old dog owner # 2: Absolutely.
Old dog owner # 1: Then I'd better sell the shar-peis.

Smart Cookie

If you think your dog can't count, try putting three dog biscuits in your pocket and feeding him two.

A Sound Investment

A woman walked into the pet store. "I haven't got much money," she told the clerk, "so I'd like to know if you've any puppies you'll let go cheap."

"I'd let them go cheep, ma'am," said the clerk, "but they prefer to go bow wow."

What Goes Around . . .

Jonathan, noted for his tact, was awakened one morning at four o'clock by his ringing telephone. "Your dog's barking, and it's keeping me awake," screamed an irate voice.

Jonathan thanked the caller and politely asked his name before hanging up.

The next morning at four o'clock, Jonathan called back his neighbor. "Sir," he said, "I don't have a dog."

Knightly News

In days of old when knights were bold, people were a lot smaller than they are today. They were so much smaller that they rode on large dogs when they couldn't obtain horses, which were quite scarce in Europe.

One dark and stormy night, as the wind blew the rain about, a squire entered a pet store to purchase a large dog for his master, the Black Knight. Unfortunately, all the shopkeeper could offer the squire was one undersize, mangy mutt. Commented the squire, "I wouldn't send a knight out on a dog like this."

Be Concise

A dog went to a Western Union office, took out a blank form, and wrote, *Woof, woof, woof, woof, woof, woof, woof, woof, woof.*

The clerk examined the paper and told the dog, "There are only nine words here. You could send another *woof* for the same cost."

"But," the dog replied, "that would be silly."

27 Lists Every Dog Lover Should Know

Forty Names for Your Dog

Bringing home a new puppy is as joyful and exciting as bringing home a baby. In both instances, you'll want to give the adorable creature the right name. According to recent polls, here's a selection of the most popular names for male and female dogs in the United States:

Males	*Females*
1. Max	1. Maggie
2. Jake	2. Molly
3. Buddy	3. Lady
4. Bailey	4. Sadie
5. Sam/Sammy	5. Lucy
6. Rocky	6. Daisy
7. Buster	7. Ginger
8. Casey	8. Ashley
9. Cody	9. Sasha
10. Duke	10. Sandy
11. Charlie	11. Dakota
12. Jack	12. Katie
13. Harley	13. Annie

14. Rusty
15. Toby
16. Murphy
17. Shelby
18. Sparky
19. Barney
20. Winston

14. Chelsea
15. Princess
16. Missy
17. Sophie
18. Baby
19. Coco
20. Tasha

Twelve Laws of Dog Territory

1. The dog is not allowed in the house.
2. The dog is allowed in the garage.
3. Okay, the dog is allowed in the house, but only in certain rooms.
4. Well, the dog is allowed in all rooms, but has to stay off the furniture.
5. The dog can get on the old furniture only.
6. Fine, the dog is allowed on all the furniture, but is not allowed to sleep with the humans on the bed.
7. Okay, the dog is allowed on the bed, but only by invitation.
8. Sigh. The dog is allowed on the bed at any time.
9. The dog can sleep on the bed, but not under the covers.
10. The dog can sleep under the covers by invitation only.
11. The dog can sleep under the covers every night.
12. Humans must ask permission to sleep under the covers with the dog.

Twenty-Two Doggie Bumper Snickers

1. Dog Is My Copilot.

2. In Dog We Trust.

3. The Four Dog Food Groups: Dry, Canned, Natural, Yours.

4. I Got Rid of My Husband. The Dog Was Allergic.

5. Dachshunds Rule! Get a Long Little Doggie.

6. Auntie Em: Hate you, Hate Kansas, Taking the Dog.—Dorothy.

7. I've Been Rejected by the Military: My Seeing Eye Dog Has Flat Feet.

8. The Dog Ate My Cliff's Notes.

9. I Neutered My Dog. Now He's a Consultant.

10. My Dog Behaves Better Than Your Kid.

11. My Schnauzer Can Beat Up Your Obedience School Honor Student.

12. We're Staying Together Because of the Dog.

13. Caution—Driver Drools Out the Window!

14. Hey, Cat! New Law—Red Light Means "Go."

15. I'd Rather Be Digging a Hole in the Backyard!

16. If You Can Read This, You're Hanging Too Far Out the Window!

17. My Dog's Gone Because I Spilled Spot Remover on Him.

18. Every Dog Has His Day, Unless He Loses His Tail. Then He Has a Weak End.

19. *Vet* Is a Four-Letter Word.

20. We Have Warm Hearts for Cold Noses.

21. Some Days You're the Dog. Some Days You're the Hydrant.

22. Editors Are to Manuscripts as Dogs Are to Fireplugs.

Nine Clues That Your Dog Has Hacked into Your E-Mail Password

1. Every time you boot up, your dog's tail starts wagging.

2. Your keyboard has traces of kibble and drool and a strange territorial scent.

3. Your mouse has teeth marks in it—and an aroma of Alpo.

4. You find you've been subscribed to strange newsgroups like www .recreational.ballchasing.

5. You receive e-mail messages from some guy named Fido.

6. Your Web browser has a new home page—http.//www.canine.com.

7. Your outbox contains hate-mail messages to Apple Computer Corp. about their release of "CyberCat."

8. Your screensaver is now a picture of Lassie and your mouse pad a picture of Rin Tin Tin.

9. Your dog is wearing carpal-tunnel braces.

Fourteen Clues That Your Dog Is Too Fat

1. The bone he dug up in the backyard is from the neck of a dinosaur.

2. You've been waiting fifteen months for her to have her dozen puppies.

3. He catches only cats that get sucked into his gravitational pull.

4. Her ginormous gut keeps the hardwood floors shiny. The dog isn't buffed, but the floors sure are.

5. When he lies around the house, he lies *around* the house.

6. She was in the Macy's Thanksgiving Day Parade, wearing ropes.

7. He has his own Zip code.

8. When she walks along the beach, the tide comes in.

9. Confused guests keep mistaking him for a beanbag chair.

10. Whenever you try to lift her, your back goes out—and your back goes out more than she does.

11. You've retrofitted the dog door with a garage door opener.

12. When your dog jumps into bed with you, you roll in his direction.

13. You've taken her for the same number of rides in the car, but your gas costs have doubled.

14. You've noticed an upsurge in collapsed furniture.

Ten Barks Heard Around the World

Lassie, Rin Tin Tin Tin, and Snoopy bark *Arf!*, *Bowwow!*, and *Woof!*, but they do that only if they are English-barking dogs. The rest of the world, it appears, doesn't hear ear-to-ear with us:

1. Brazilian   *Au-au!*

2. Chinese   *Wang-wang!*

3. French   *Gnaf-gnaf!*

4. German   *Wau wau!*

5. Hebrew   *Hav-hav!*

6. Japanese   *Wan-wan!*

7. Russian   *Gav-gav!*

8. Swahili   *Hu-hu-hu-huuu!*

9. Swedish   *Voff-voff!*

10. And 50,000,000 Italians are convinced their dogs bark like Bing Crosby—*Boo-boo!*

Twenty Canine Palindromes

A palindrome is a word, like *level;* a compound, like *pooch coop;* or a sentence, like STEP ON NO PETS that communicates the same message when the letters of which it is composed are read in reverse order. Cast your eyes upon the twenty most elegant sentence palindromes that include dogs:

REX: I'M A MIXER.

SALT A PUP, ATLAS.

PAT A DOG. GOD—A TAP.

STARK RABID, I BARK, "RATS!"

A DOG? A PANIC IN A PAGODA!

GODS RIDICULE LUCID IRS DOG.

GOD! NATE BIT A TIBETAN DOG.

TEN ALPO DOGS GO DO PLANET.

GOD! A NOTE, O POET, ON A DOG.

DRAW PUPIL'S PUP'S LIP UPWARD.

"DOG," SIDES REVERSED, IS "GOD."

FOOL A POOR DOG. GO DROOP ALOOF.

GODDESSES, SO PAT A POSSESSED DOG.

RISE, SIR LAPDOG——GOD, PAL. RISE, SIR.

DOG AS A DEVIL NEVER EVEN LIVED AS A GOD.

GOD! A RED NUGGET! A FAT EGG UNDER A DOG!

DID I STEP ON DOG DOO? GOOD GOD! NO PETS! I DID!

"WARDEN IN A CAP," MAC'S PUP, SCAMP, A CANINE DRAW.

EVA, CAN I STAB ONE MAN'S DOG? GODS NAME NO BATS IN A CAVE.

ARE WE NOT DRAWN ONWARD, PUP, DRAWN ONWARD TO NEW ERA?

Whoever said
you can't buy happiness
forgot little puppies.
—*Gene Hill*

Love for Sale

You can't buy loyalty, they say.
I bought it, though, the other day.
You can't buy friendship, tried and true.
Well just the same, I bought that, too.

I made my bid, and on the spot
Bought love and faith and a whole job lot
Of happiness and a trusting heart
That gave devotion from the start.

If you think these things are not for sale,
Buy a brown-eyed puppy with a stump for a tail.

Priceless Love

A farmer had some puppies he needed to sell. He painted a sign advertising the four pups and set about nailing it to a post on the edge of his yard.

As he was driving the last nail, he felt a tug on his overalls. He looked down into the eyes of a little boy. "Mister," the boy said, "I want to buy one of your puppies."

"Well," said the farmer, as he rubbed the sweat off the back of his neck. "These puppies come from fine parents and cost a good deal of money."

The boy dropped his head for a moment. Then reaching deep into his pocket, he pulled out a handful of change and held it up to the farmer. "I've got thirty-nine cents. Is that enough to take a look?"

"Sure," said the farmer, and with that he let out a whistle. "Here, Dolly!" he called. Out from the doghouse and down the ramp ran Dolly, followed by four little balls of fur. The boy pressed his face against the chain link fence. His eyes danced with delight.

As the dogs made their way to the fence, the boy noticed something else stirring inside the doghouse. Slowly another little ball appeared, this one noticeably smaller. Down the ramp it slid clumsily. Then the little pup began hobbling toward the others, doing its best to catch up. "I want that one," the little boy said, pointing to the runt.

The farmer knelt down at the boy's side and said, "Son, you don't want that puppy. He will never be able to run and play with you like these other dogs will."

The little boy stepped back from the fence, reached down, and rolled up one leg of his trousers. He revealed a steel brace running down both sides of his leg, attaching itself to a specially made shoe. Looking back up at the farmer, he said, "You see sir, I don't run too well myself, and he will need someone who understands."

Brushing tears from his cheeks, the farmer reached down and picked up the little pup and carefully handed it to the little boy.

"How much?" asked the boy.

"No charge," answered the farmer. "There's no charge for love."

How Much Is That Doggie in the Want Ad?

The following want ad appeared in a local newspaper:

SINGLE BLACK FEMALE Seeks Male companionship, ethnicity unimportant. I'm a svelte good-looking girl who LOVES to play. I love long walks in the woods. Riding in your pickup truck. Hunting. Camping. Fishing trips. Cozy winter nights spent lying by the fire. Candlelight dinners will have me eating out of your hand. Rub me the right way and watch me respond! I'll be at the front door when you get home from work, wearing only what nature gave me! Kiss me and I'm yours! Call 555-1234 and ask for Daisy.

The phone number was for the Humane Society, and Daisy was an eight-week-old black Labrador retriever!

The following classified ads are not so clever and are presented here exactly as they originally appeared:

- The license fee for altered dogs with a certificate will be three dollars and for pets owned by seniors who have not been altered the fee will be a dollar-fifty.

- The Macon County Humane Society offers a free spay/neutering to senior citizens if they adopt an animal out of the animal shelter.

- Springer spaniel female whose owner desires to mate w/ beautiful male, liver & white Springer with AKC thoroughbred papers.

- FOR SALE: Great Dames

- FOR SALE: Two female Boston terrier puppies, seven weeks old. Perfect markings. Call 555-1234. Leave mess.

- FOR SALE: Dog. Eats anything and is fond of children.

- FOR SALE: Eight puppies from an German shepherd and an Alaskan Hussy.

- FOR SALE: Purebred miniature collie puppies. Tri-color and sable. Can see both parents.

- TO GIVE AWAY: 10-year-old Shiatsu cross. Good with children and other animals.

- LOST: Deaf golden Labrador. Doesn't answer to name "Winnie."

- LOST: small apricot poodle. Reward. Neutered. Like one of the family.

- LOST: Male dog. Needs medication. Owner very worried, neutered and declawed.

- LOST: 2-year-old brown male Datsun. Very well behaved and friendly.

- Dog training: Private and group classes will teach your family and pet off-leash obedience.

- FOUND: Dirty white dog. Looks like rat. Been out awhile. Better be reward.

I am his Highness' dog at Kew;
Pray tell me, sir,
whose dog are you?

—*Alexander Pope*

Old Dog Tray

Old dog Tray's ever faithful;
Grief cannot drive him away;
He's gentle, he is kind,
I'll never, never find
A better friend than old dog Tray.

—*Stephen Foster*

The Lost Dog

I saw a little dog today,
And oh, that dog was lost.
He risked his anguished puppy life
With every street he crossed.

He shrank away from outstretched hands.
He winced at every hail.
Against the city's bigness he
Looked very small and frail.

Distrust lay in his tortured eyes,
His body shook with fright;
(I wondered when he'd eaten last—
And where he'd slept at night!)

I whistled, and I followed him,
And hoped that he might guess
That all my soul reached out to him,
And offered friendliness!

So many times I have been lost,
And lonely and afraid!
I followed through the crowded streets,
I followed—and I prayed.

And then the God of little things,
Who knows when sparrows fall,
Put trust into the puppy's heart
And made him heed my call.
　　　　　　　　—Margaret E. Sangster

The Dog's Cold Nose

When Noah, perceiving 'twas time to embark,
Persuaded the creatures to enter the Ark,
The dog, with a friendliness truly sublime,
Assisted in herding them two at a time.
He drove in the elephants, zebras, and gnus
Until they were packed like a box full of screws—
The cat in the cupboard, the mouse on the shelf,
The bug in the crack; then he backed in himself.

But such was the lack of available space
He couldn't tuck all of him into the place;
So after the waters had flooded the plain
And down from the heavens fell blankets of rain,
He stood with his muzzle thrust out through the door
The whole forty days of that terrible pour!
Because of which drenching, zoologists hold,
The nose of a healthy dog always is cold!

—Arthur Guiterman

A New Day

All in the town were still asleep
When the sun came up with a shout and a leap.
In the lonely streets, unseen by man,
A little dog danced, and the day began.

—Rupert Brooke

30 Nursery Rhyme Dogs

A dog is the only thing
on earth that loves you
more than he loves himself.

—*Josh Billings*

Dogs are so much a part of our lives that they live in our children's nursery rhymes. Supply the missing lines in each classic verse from our childhood. Answers follow.

1. High diddle, diddle,
   The cat and the fiddle,
   The cow jumped over the moon;

   _____

   To see such craft,
   And the dish ran away with the spoon.

2. Old Mother Hubbard
   Went to the cupboard

   _____;

   But when she came there
   The cupboard was bare
   And so the poor dog had none.

3. I sent a letter to my love
   And on the way I dropped it,

   _____

   And put it in his pocket.

4. _____

   Oh where, oh where can he be?
   With his ears cut short and his tail cut long,
   Oh where, oh where is he?

5. What are little boys made of?

   _____

   That's what little boys are made of !
   What are little girls made of?
   Sugar and spice and all things nice—
   That's what little girls are made of.

6. Bow, wow, wow,

   _____?

   Little Tom Tinker's dog,
   Bow wow wow.

Answers

1. The little dog laughed 2. To fetch her poor dog a bone 3. A little puppy picked it up 4. Oh where, oh where has my little dog gone? 5. Snips and snails, and puppy dogs' tails 6. Whose dog art thou

31 Doggerel Haiku

Dogs' lives are too short.
Their only fault, really.
—*Agnes Sligh Turnbull*

I love my master.
Thus I perfume myself with
This long-rotten squirrel.

I lie belly-up
In the sunshine, happier than
You will ever be.

I bite squeaky toys:
Squeak squeak squeak squeak squeak squeak squeak
Squeak squeak squeak squeak squeak.

I sound the alarm!
Paperboy comes to kill us all!
Look! Look! Look! Look! Look!

I sound the alarm!
Mailman comes to kill us all!
Look! Look! Look! Look! Look!

I sound the alarm!
Meterman comes to kill us all!
Look! Look! Look! Look! Look!

I lift my leg and
Wiz on each bush. Hello, Spot.
Sniff this and weep.

How do I love thee?
The ways are numberless as
My hairs on the rug.

My human is home!
I'm so ecstatic I have
Made a puddle here.

I hate my choke chain.
Look, world, they are strangling me!
Ack! Ack! Ack! Ack! Ack!

Sleeping here, my chin
On your foot. No greater bliss . . .
Except catching cats.

Look in my eyes and
Deny it. No human could
Love you as I do.

Dig under fence. Why?
Because it's there. Because it's
There. Because it's there.

I am your best friend,
Always, and especially
When you are eating.

32 An Enduring Elegy

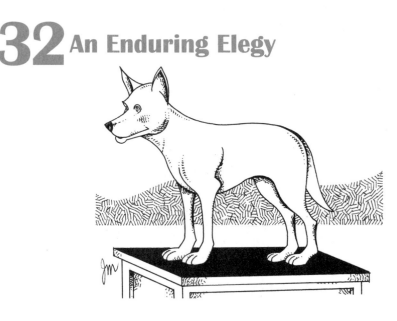

**The bond with a dog
is as lasting as the ties
of this earth can ever be.**
—*Konrad Lorenz*

In 1870, a Sedalia, Missouri, attorney named George Graham Vest represented a client whose foxhound, Old Drum, had been viciously killed by a human neighbor. Vest, who went on to become a U.S. senator, concluded his argument with the following argument. In a tear-drenched courtroom he won the case:

"Gentlemen of the jury, the one absolutely unselfish friend that a man can have in this selfish world, the one that never deserts him, the one that never proves ungrateful or treacherous, is his dog.

"A man's dog stands by him in prosperity and in poverty, in health and in sickness. He will sleep on the cold ground where the wintry winds blow, and the snow drives fiercely, if only he may be near his master's side. He will kiss the hand that has no food to offer; he will lick the sores and wounds that come in encounter with the roughness of the world. He guards the sleep of his pauper master as if he were a prince.

"Gentlemen of the jury, when all other friends desert, he remains. When riches take wings and reputation falls to pieces, he is as constant in his love as the sun in its journey through the heavens. If misfortune drives the master forth an outcast in the world, friendless and homeless, the faithful dog asks no higher privilege than that of accompanying him to guard against danger, to fight against his enemies.

"And when the last scene of all comes, and death takes the master in its embrace, and his body is laid away in the cold ground, no matter if all other friends pursue their way, there by the graveside will the noble dog be found, his head between his paws, his eyes sad, but open in alert watchfulness, faithful and true, even in death."

33 The Quotable Dog

Humorists on Dogs

If you pick up a starving dog and make him prosperous, he will not bite you; that is the principal difference between a man and a dog.

—*Mark Twain*

Outside of a dog, a book is a man's best friend. Inside of a dog, it's too dark to read.

—*Groucho Marx*

The average dog is a nicer person than the average person.

—*Andy Rooney*

Dogs feel very strongly that they should always go with you in the car, in case the need should arise for them to bark violently at nothing right in your ear.

—*Dave Barry*

You can say any fool thing to a dog, and the dog will give you this look that says, "My God, you're right! I NEVER would've thought of that!"

—*Dave Barry*

Dogs need to sniff the ground; it's how they keep abreast of current events. The ground is a giant dog newspaper, containing all kinds of late-breaking dog news items.

—*Dave Barry*

Dachshunds are the ideal dogs for small children as they are already stretched and pulled to such a length that the child cannot do much harm one way or another.

—*Robert Benchley*

Dogs lead a nice life. You never see a dog with a wristwatch.

—*George Carlin*

My husband and I are either going to buy a dog or have a child. We can't decide whether to ruin our carpet or ruin our lives.

—*Rita Rudner*

We've begun to long for the pitter-patter of little feet, so we bought a dog. It's cheaper, and you get more feet.

—*Rita Rudner*

I got a wirehaired terrier that wouldn't bark, so I had him rewired for sound.

—*Red Skelton*

I know that dogs are pack animals, but it is difficult to imagine a pack of standard poodles. And if there was such a thing as a pack of standard poodles, where would they rove to? Bloomingdale's?

—*Yvonne Clifford*

I have a dog that's half pit bull and half poodle. Not much of a guard dog, but a vicious gossip.

—*Craig Shoemaker*

Life is like a dogsled team. If you ain't the lead dog, the scenery never changes.

—*P. J. O'Rourke*

I tell you, my dog is lazy. He don't chase cars. He sits on the curb and takes down license plate numbers.

—*Rodney Dangerfield*

If you don't want your dog to have bad breath, do what I do: Pour a little Lavoris in the toilet.

—*Jay Leno*

I hope if dogs ever take over the world and choose a king, they just don't go by size, because I bet there are some Chihuahuas with some good ideas.

—*Jack Handey*

My dog is worried about the economy because Alpo is up to 99 cents a can. That's almost $7.00 in dog money.

—*Joe Weinstein*

I've heard that dogs are man's best friend. That explains where men are getting their hygiene tips.

—*Kelly Maguire*

I once had a dog who really believed he was man's best friend. He kept borrowing money from me.

—*Gene Perret*

They say a dog is man's best friend, but I don't buy it. How many of your friends have had you neutered?

—*Larry Reeb*

My friend George walked his dog, all at once. Walked it from Boston to Fort Lauderdale, and said, "Now you're done."

—*Steven Wright*

Chihuahua, there's a waste of dog food. Looks like a dog that is still far away.

—*Billiam Coronel*

I have a dog, and I've trained him to go on the paper. But he won't wait until I've finished reading it.

—*Richard Jeni*

I have always thought of a dog lover as a dog who was in love with another dog.

—*James Thurber*

My mother was a ventriloquist. She could throw her voice. So for ten years I thought the dog was telling me to kill my father.

—*Wendy Liebman*

I was in Alaska. I was there for two days and six nights. It was so cold I saw a dog wearing a cat.

—*Wendy Liebman*

But Seriously . . .

You become responsible, forever, for what you have tamed.

—*Antoine de Saint-Exupéry*

A house or an apartment becomes a home when you add one set of four legs, a happy tail, and that indescribable measure of love that we call a dog.

—*Roger Caras*

We are alone, absolutely alone on this chance planet and, amid all the forms of life that surround us, not one, excepting the dog, has made an alliance with us.

—*Maurice Maeterlinck*

My goal in life is to become as wonderful as my dog thinks I am. It reminds me that I have a long way to go to even come close to being as wonderful as my dog thinks I am—or at least as wonderful as I think she thinks I am.

—*Tony Green*

Acquiring a dog may be the only opportunity a human ever has to choose a relative.

—*Mordecai Segal*

Living with a dog is easy—like living with an idealist.

—*H. L. Mencken*

No matter how little money and how few possessions you own, having a dog makes you rich.

—*Louis Sabin*

There is no psychiatrist in the world like a puppy licking your face.

—*Ben Williams*

No one can fully understand the meaning of love unless he is owned by a dog.

—Gene Hill

Ever consider what they must think of us? I mean, here we come back from a grocery store with the most amazing haul—chicken, pork, half a cow. They must think we're the greatest hunters on earth!

—Ann Tyler

There's nothing like a cold nose and a wet tongue to get one started in the morning.

—Brad Anderson

No one who has not, upon returning from any absence, long or short, been greeted by a loving dog can understand what devotion is. There is no affection like it anywhere on earth, and those for whom it is the heart's balm understand what a love elixir is.

—Carolyn G. Heilbrun

Not the least hard thing to bear when they go away from us, these quiet friends, is that they carry away with them so many years of our own lives.

—John Galsworthy

I guess you don't really own a dog. You rent them, and you have to be thankful that you had a long lease.

—Author Unknown

There is always a barrier between me and any man or woman who does not like dogs.

—Ellen Glasgow

To his dog, every man is Napoleon. Hence the constant popularity of dogs.

—*Aldous Huxley*

Don't accept your dog's admiration as conclusive evidence that you are wonderful.

—*Ann Landers*

Old dogs, like old shoes, are comfortable. They might be a bit out of shape and a little worn around the edges, but they fit well.

—*Bonnie Wilcox*

The dog was created specially for children. He is a god of frolic.

—*Henry Ward Beecher*

Do not make the mistake of treating your dogs like humans or they will treat you like dogs.

—*Martha Scott*

When a man's best friend is his dog, that dog has a problem.

—*Edward Abbey*

Saving just one dog won't change the world, but surely the world will change for that one dog.

—*Author Unknown*

Dogs are our link to paradise. They don't know evil or jealousy or discontent. To sit with a dog on a hillside on a glorious afternoon is to be back in Eden, where doing nothing was not boring; it was peace.

—*Milan Kundera*

The one place to bury a good dog is in the heart of his master.

—*Ben Hur Lampman*